Asli Punjabi Khanna

Spiderwize
Remus House
Coltsfoot Drive
Woodston
Peterborough
PE2 9BF

www.spiderwize.com

# asli punjabi khanna
# {Real Punjabi food}

Simplest cookery book of the year

# By
# Nirmala Singh

Dishes made in the Punjabi household daily

Curries were popular in the Punjab at first. Now there is a take away /curry house in nearly every town or city. It has become one of the most popular dish served {chicken curry} {chicken vindaloo} WHATEVER!

But the difference you will find in this cook book, to others, is that I use only pure fresh ingredients, everything is authentic. The dishes in this book, are the ones every Punjabi household cooks on a regular basis.

The dishes are simple and easy to prepare, look good and of course taste delicious. I am sure you will be licking your fingers after each meal.

I have two reasons for writing this cookery book one is for anyone as young as 12 to learn how to cook Punjabi meals. I myself started very young. At the age of 12, I could make a three course meal. It wasn't difficult, because I come from a very traditional family where the first thing a girl is taught, is how to cook; therefore it came natural to me, plus the fact I enjoy cooking.

Girls these days, have no patience at all, being taught by parents, so I'm hoping this cookery book will inspire them to pick it up and start cooking and surprise their parents.

The other reason is that I want my granddaughters to learn from it. I only came into believing I could actually do this, [write a cookery book] is because of friends and collegues at work. I often took curries, I had cooked to school, my friends would ask for recipes and jokingly I would say 'you have to wait for my cookery book to be published' and now it's become a reality. I owe it to my school colleagues for making it possible.

I have never used measuring equipment, for the only reason, that they were never used in Indian cooking from the beginning. All measurements were done by the eye.

Although I have given rough guides to how you can measure. It is much easier using cups of flour, half a bag of sugar, a cup of rice or the tip of table spoon. See picture pg12 for examples. It comes out perfect. I give you my guarantee.

I hope you will enjoy cooking, and have luxury meals, that would cost a fortune from a take-away, will now, cost you a few pounds, for the whole family. You must remember that once you buy ingredients for one dish, the ingredients will go a long way, as you only need small amounts.

Salt was the hardest to measure but I have used a teaspoon or a spoonful as a guide for beginners, but the more you cook you will be able to master the skill, just by your eye and be able to judge just by looking at the quantity of what you are cooking. See pg12 of examples. I myself have always used the tip of table spoon. I find it's easier to judge. Once you start using a table spoon for hand eye measuring, you will soon become and expert. You will find that you will be perfecting it with each dish.

{Practice makes perfect} It is better to use less salt because it's easier to correct, by adding more after tasting it. But if you happen to add too much you can correct it also; by adding a whole potato to your dish it will reduce the salt.

Nirmala Singh

I would like to dedicate this book to all our elders, especially my dad Aujager Singh Jagga and mum Inder Kaur, who sacrificed their own happiness to give us a better life.

I would also like to dedicate it to my brothers Dalbir Singh, Baldave Singh, Pritam Singh; sisters Pritam, Ratan and Kamala.

# Contents

## Sweet Dishes, Healthy Drinks and Snacks

## Breads

## Daals

# Rice Dishes

# Curries

# WHAT IS BEST?

## Potatoes

When cooking potatoes in curries, it is best to use quality not quantity.
I find Maris Piper or King Edward potatoes the best. They cook to a nice and fluffy texture, also cook in equally when adding other veg, to a curry e.g. cauliflower or aubergine.
They are also great for samosas and pakoras. Some potatoes contain lots of moisture, when used in curries, it makes a lot of difference to the time it takes to cook and how the curry turns out.

## Rice

When cooking rice in curries, sweet dishes, or plain boiled rice .It is best to use Basmati or long grain rice only. This type of rice, cooks to a fluffy texture, leaving each grain separate.
The trick to have separated grain of rice each time is to, rinse it a few times till water runs clear, this gets rid of all the starch.

## Chapatti flour

When making chapattis' it is best to use quality white flour. I find that white chapatti flour is best, because roti stays soft for quite a while.  It is also great for making a prantha {flat fried bread} Brown chapatti flour, is very tasty, but roti goes hard as soon as roti gets cold.
Although some believe brown flour is healthier than white. Try and judge for yourself!!

## Meat

When cooking meat, try and use fresh meat, chicken, lamb, pork or other.
It is best to buy enough for a dish; and taste the difference, although there is nothing wrong with frozen meat. It is also a hassle to defrost, and if not defrosted properly it could give you food poisoning.
Also, when cooking diced meat always add a piece of bone to give the sauce some rich texture.

## Vegetables

When cooking vegetables. If you have time, it is best to use fresh. But alternatively you can use frozen. Peas, and mix vegetables cook like fresh. Tinned chick peas and beans cook like fresh.

## Tinned tomatoes

To give your curries a rich texture in the sauce depends on the tinned tomatoes you use. It is best to use rich Italian tinned tomatoes, it instantly gives the sauce the correct balance and also helps blend other spices accurately. In vegetarian dishes it is best to use fresh tomatoes, fresh tomatoes keep the vegetables moist, but not wet.

## Turn page for examples;

As you begin to cook curries, you will master the skill of using a tablespoon for all measurements. By putting salt or spice at the tip of a tablespoon and by looking at the quantity of what you are cooking. It will be perfect each time. Although I have used a teaspoon, just to make it easier for beginners. As less can be corrected.
So once you have made a curry from this book, you might find it is too mild or too hot. After a few tries you will perfect it, and surprise yourself.

{Practice Makes Perfect}

# Main ingredients to make...

## Spiced dishes:

Salt
Huldi
Chilli powder
Masala
Jeera
Jiven
Tandoori masala
Flaked chillies
5Mix masala -
(large cardamom, cloves,
cinnamon sticks, coriander
seeds and jeera seeds)
Food colouring - red/orange
Tinned tomatoes
Garlic fresh / frozen
Ginger fresh / frozen
Oil / Clarified margarine
Bay leaves
Fresh coriander
Fresh mint
Onions

## Sweet dishes:

Fresh unsalted butter
Orange food colouring
Pistachios
Flaked almonds
Whole almonds
Sugar

# Utensils that are a must in Asian cooking

**Tava** (flat pan for chappatis'-roti)
Easily bought from any Asian food wholesale /store

**Deep Karai** (two handle deep pan)
Best for making, sagg, dry spinach, methi alloo, (fenugreek and potato)
To fry puris, naan bread, and matia (biscuits)

**Non stick wok**
To fry pakoras and samosas.

**Thantha** (round spatula with holes)

It makes a lot of difference if you have the right utensils especially when frying or making crispy sagg.

**Heavy bottom deep pan**
For daals, ronghi {kidney beans}

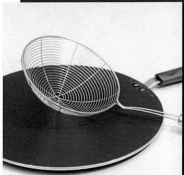

**Mortar and pestle**
For grinding, garlic, ginger or making small amounts of chutney.
Alternatively you could use a mini chopper.

Any tricky words see glossary.

# Clarifying Margarine & Butter

## Clarifying margarine:

I have always used clarified margarine in my pastries and saggs (fenugreek and potato) Clarified butter is best used for sweet dishes.

## How to clarify margarine:

- Place a block of premium brand margarine in a pan, on low heat; blocks are better because they contain minimum water.
  Margarine from a tub will take longer and may also burn, whilst heating because it contains more water than the margarine.
- Make sure heat is very low or it will boil over or start to bubble up, and could easily spill on you.
- {Tip: It is best to use the hob that is at the back, because should any accident occur it wouldn't be as severe as it would if it is on the front hob.}
- Once it is melted keep it on low heat for a further 3-4 minutes, then pour it into a casserole or Pyrex dish and let it set.
- After it is set (couple of hours or overnight) pierce a hole in the margarine with a skewer or something sharp, turn it sideways and release the water.

## How to clarify butter:

- Place block of butter on very low heat and slowly let it melt for 2-3 minutes as butter is not like margarine and can burn easily.
- Once melted use a tea strainer and strain away the froth on top and let the rest cool and now it's ready to use for sweet dishes. {Tip: always use unsalted butter}

# GRINDING YOUR VERY OWN MASALA

To make your own masala is so very easy, all you will need:

1 small packet of black peppercorn – 300g
1 packet of 5 mix masala - 400g*

- Mix all ingredients in a bowl.
- In smaller quantities grind it in a coffee grinder it's as simple as that, but you will see the difference it makes to all Punjabi cooking.

The ready ground masala that you can buy makes the curries very dark and bland, giving it no real purpose other than to think you've added everything needed to make the curry.

But the masala, you grind, will add the extra kick needed in making curries and all spice dishes authentic.

*Jeera, bay leaves, coriander seeds, moti lachi, cloves and cinnamon stick.
For the names of different seeds look in the glossary see pg122.

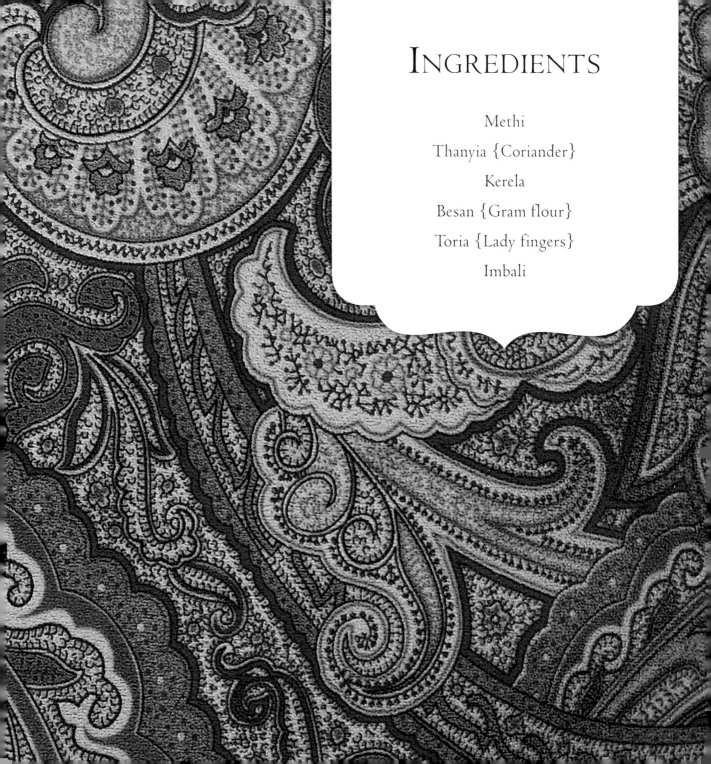

# Ingredients

Methi

Thanyia {Coriander}

Kerela

Besan {Gram flour}

Toria {Lady fingers}

Imbali

# METHI

Methi is an Eastern spring green. It is best when cooked from fresh. It is also best to pluck the leaves close to the stems, then chop and cook them with potatoes.

By adding too much of the stems it might become a bigger dish {quantity} but it affects the taste, also the stems get stuck in your teeth.

You can use dried methi to garnish dishes; it gives a totally different aroma and taste to any curry.

It is also great for adding to Pakora, it gives it extra crispiness.

# THANYIA {CORIANDER}

Thanyia is an aromatic herb great for garnishing, equally so when cooked like sagg.

Try cooking a bunch of thanyia {coriander} exactly like methi alloo {see pg46} it tastes amazing.

It is also great when added to pakora mix or when making chutnies.

# Kerela

Kerela is an Eastern vegetable. It is an acquired taste; you either like it or hate it.

It has a very bitter taste, but if cooked correctly you can hardly taste the bitterness. The way this vegetable is prepared, makes all the difference.

The best way, is to get a potato peeler, and gently peel off the bumps on the kerela, that is where most of the bitterness sits.

Rinse with cold water and leave to drain, before frying.

# Besan {gram flour}

Besan is a flour made from chick peas, used for many purposes in Asian cooking.

It is used on it's own for curry. It is used for batter mix, pakora mix.

It is also used for making misi roti, a chapatti made with other ingredients {see pg106}

# TORIA {LADY FINGERS}

Toria is a different kind of vegetable, if not washed and prepared properly, it will be a total disaster.

So to begin with, run toria under cold water. Next with a paper towel or clean tea towel, dry the toria. Next, top and tail them, then slice them in half then again down the middle.

The reason for washing and drying them before cutting is to prevent it releasing a sticky substance, which makes it harder and very messy to handle.

You can also slice them round like a cucumber.

# IMBALI

Imbali is a sweet and sour fruit, mostly used for chutneys and sauces.

You can buy imbali seedless or dry. I prefer dry imbali, it is less messy to handle when making chutney in the processor.

{Tip: When using dry always press out the stones, to prevent damaging your processor.}

But the wet seedless imbali is better for making watery sauces.

# Vegitarian dishes

Alloo Gobi {cauliflower and potato}

Alloo Bataue {aubergine and potato}

Alloo Bataue Fried {aubergine and potato}

Alloo Matar {potatoes with peas in sauce}

Chana Puri {chick peas with puri}

Boonia Saag {crispy spring cabbage}

Toria {lady fingers}

Spicy Beans

Radish Saag Wraps

Alloo Gajara {carrots with potatoes}

Partha {pulped aubergine}

Methi Alloo {fenugreek with potatoes}

Kolma Sagg {pureed spinach}

Dishes Made From Leftover Spinach

Kerela Alloo {Kerala with potatoes}

Jiven Alloo {potatoes}

Samosas

Broccoli

# ALLOO GOBI {CAULIFLOWER AND POTATO}

## Method:

- Wash and drain cauliflower and potatoes.
- In a pan add oil, cauliflower and potatoes keep turning them in the oil for at least 3/4mins, keeping pan on low heat, at this point the cauliflower and potatoes will slightly change colour.
- Add the rest of the ingredients except masala, coriander and butter.
- Lastly, add the masala mix well, bring to boiling point and simmer for 15/20 minutes or until potatoes have cooked through and break easily.
- {Tip: Add butter soon as you take it off the heat as it will give it a creamy taste to Gobi Alloo, finish off by sprinkling coriander}

{Any tricky words look in glossary}

## Ingredients

### SERVES 4

1 Average size cauliflower cut into small pieces

2 large potatoes cut into small pieces

1 tablespoon of oil

1 level teaspoon salt

½ a teaspoon chilli powder

½ a teaspoon huldi

1 spoonful masala

2 tinned tomatoes and half the juice

2 green chillies finely chopped

Small piece of ginger chopped

Coriander for garnish

Dollop of butter

# ALLOO BATAUE {POTATO AND AUBERGINE}

## Method:

- Wash and drain the aubergine and potatoes.
- In a pan add oil, aubergine and potatoes keep turning them in the oil for at least 3/4mins, keeping pan on low heat, at this point the aubergine and potatoes will slightly change colour.
- Add the rest of the ingredients except masala, coriander and butter.
- Lastly add the masala, mix well, bring to boiling point and simmer for 15/20 minutes or until potatoes have cooked through and break easily.

{Tip: Add butter soon as you take it off the heat as it will give it a creamy taste to Alloo Bataue, finish off by sprinkling coriander}

{Any tricky words look in glossary}

## Ingredients

### SERVES 4

1 Average size aubergine cut into small pieces

2 large potatoes cut into small pieces

1 tablespoon of oil

1 teaspoon salt

½ a teaspoon chilli powder

½ a teaspoon huldi

1 spoonful of masala

2 tinned tomatoes and half the juice

2 green chillies finely chopped

Small piece of ginger chopped

Coriander for garnish

Dollop of butter

# ALLOO BATAUE FRIED
{FRIED AUBERGINE AND POTATO WEDGES }

## Method:

- Fry potatoes and drain in a large sieve, transfer them onto kitchen paper
- Next fry aubergines and repeat process
- Once drained, spread onto kitchen paper gently mix
- Sprinkle salt, chilli flakes and masala
- Ready to eat in a roti wrap.

{To make a wrap see pg104}

## Ingredients
### MAKES 4

2 large potatoes peeled and cut into wedges

5 /6 baby aubergines sliced into 4 pieces long ways

Salt to taste

A fair pinch of chilli flakes

A fair pinch of masala

Oil for deep frying

# ALLOO MATAR {POTATOES WITH PEAS IN SAUCE}

## Method:

- In a pan add oil and onions, fry until golden brown
- Next, add potatoes and coat with mixture. Add tomatoes, salt and green chillies.
- Mix well, add ginger, huldi, chilli powder and masala
- Stir, fusing all ingredients together
- Next add peas and water, bring to boil and simmer for 10-15 minutes or until potatoes are cooked through.
- Garnish with coriander and add butter to give dish a creamy finish. Serve with freshly made buttered roti.
- Roti can be served buttered or plain

## Ingredients

### SERVES 4

1 Large onion finely chopped

2 Medium sized potatoes cut into bite size chunks

1 cup frozen peas

1 level teaspoon salt

1 level teaspoon chilli powder

1 level teaspoon huldi

2 tomatoes from a tin and half the sauce

2 green chillies finely chopped

1½ table spoon of oil

Small piece of ginger in thin slices

1 teaspoon masala

1 pint water

Fresh coriander

Dollop of butter

# Chana puri {chick peas and puri}

## Method:

- In a karai, add oil, onions and fry till golden brown add tomatoes and juice, salt, chilli powder, green chillies, ginger, and huldi, mix well, keep mixture on low heat at all times to prevent it from sticking.
- Next, take a masher and mash all mixture to smooth it out.
- {Tip: You can cool mixture, blend it in a blender and pour it back into karai}
- Next, add ¾ of the chickpeas to mixture, with a masher, mash the other ¼ of chickpeas and add to karai, add 1 cup of water add masala and bring to boiling point, leave on heat for a further 30 seconds.
- Finish off with a sprinkle of freshly chopped coriander.
- Serve with hot puri, or paturae see pg114 and 120.

{Any tricky words look in glossary}

## Ingredients

### SERVES 4

4 tins of chickpeas

2large onions finely chopped

1 level teaspoon salt

½ teaspoon chilli powder

1 or 2 green chillies finely chopped

Small piece ginger finely chopped

½ teaspoon huldi

1 ½ tablespoon oil

2/3 tomatoes from a tin and half the juice

1 spoonful masala

1 cup of water

Coriander for garnish

# Boonia Sagg {Crispy spring cabbage}

## Method:

- In karai heat oil, add cabbage, salt and ginger cover with foil
- Leave on gas, low heat for 30 mins regularly checking it's not sticking to karai
- Once cabbage has wilted, check by taking a piece of the cabbage and pressing it with your finger
- If it rubs apart easily, it is almost done, put heat up to full, and dry rest of the water
- Once it's sticking to pan and looks like its burning keep turning it.
- Add green chillies and chilli flakes, ready to eat with cold chapattis.

{Tip: Small fried potatoes or fried bacon bits can be added to the sagg}

{Any tricky words look in glossary}

32

## Ingredients

### SERVES 4

1 bag of spring cabbage/ washed and finely chopped

2 green chillies finely chopped

½ a teaspoon salt

1 teaspoon of chilli flakes

Small piece of ginger cut in thin strips

1 tablespoon of oil

# TORIA {LADY FINGERS}

## Method:

- In a deep frying pan separately fry toria, potatoes and onions, drain them each using a large sieve or colander.
- In a karai or deep frying pan, put drained ingredients, add tomatoes, chilli flakes, salt, green chillies ginger and masala, gently turn and mix, keep on very low heat until the tomatoes have softened and mixed in, giving dish a little moisture.
- Garnish with coriander, serve with lentils and plain boiled rice with home made chutney.

  {Tip: Always wash and dry toria whole, because they will become sticky, if you cut them before washing them, making it messy to handle. Slice each one through the middle, if there are any black bits discard that one, because it will have some kind of bug in it}

## Ingredients

SERVES 3/4

20 Toria {ladyfingers} washed and dried

3 Large onions finely sliced

2 Fresh tomatoes

2 Green chillies finely chopped

Small piece of ginger chopped

½teaspoon salt

1 large potato peeled and cut into wedges

1teaspoon masala

1 level teaspoon chilly flakes

½ teaspoon huldi

Oil for frying

Coriander for garnish

# Spicy Beans

## Method:

- In a frying pan, fry onions until soft.
- Add water and cook for a further minute stirring all the time.
- Next, add salt, huldi, chilli flakes and masala mix well.
- Finally, add beans bring to boil, and ready to serve.

## Ingredients

### SERVES 2

2 tin of beans

Spoonful oil

Small onion finely diced

Large pinch of salt

1 green chilli finely chopped

1 level teaspoon masala

Pinch of chilli flakes

½ cup of water

36

# TANGY POTATOES

## Method:

- In a pan heat oil, add all ingredients except coriander
- Next, bring to boiling point, cover with foil and lower the heat to very low
- Keep pan on heat for 15/20 minutes until potatoes break easily
- Garnish with coriander
- {Tip: Serve with cold or hot roti, both taste equally delicious}

## Ingredients

### SERVES 4

Tablespoon oil

2 large  potatoes diced

½ teaspoon salt

½teaspoon chilli flakes

1 green chilli finely chopped

1 teaspoon masala

¾tin of rich tomatoes and most of the sauce

Fresh coriander for garnish

# Radish sagg wraps

## Method:

Cooking time 10/15 minutes.

- Fill a large bowl with cold water and place whole radishes, soak for few seconds and then shake, drain water and repeat a few times.
  This method of washing radishes releases all the soil with very little effort.
- Next, chop the stalks very thinly, cut the radish into slices.
- In a karai, add oil and onions, fry till soft. Add radishes and greens, salt, green chilli, ginger and cover.
- As the water releases from the sagg and onions it will help cook it.
  When the water has evaporated, lift the lid and add chilli flakes.
- Make 4 rotis place a 2/3 spoonfuls in roti and make a wrap.

  {Tip: Rotis made the night before, taste even better with radish sagg}

  {Tip: Left over rotis should always be wrapped in foil to keep them from going hard}

## Ingredients

### 4 WRAPS

2 /3 bunches of radish with all the greens finely chopped

2 medium size onions sliced thinly

Pinch of salt

1 green chilli finely chopped

Big pinch of chilli flakes

4/5 very thin strips of fresh ginger

Tablespoon of oil

# Alloo Gajara {carrots with potatoes}

## Method:

- In a pan add oil, onions, and garlic, fry till soft. Add carrots and potatoes and spoon them for 3/4 minutes.
- Next, add rest of ingredients except butter, mix well.
- Bring veg to boiling point, then lower the heat to very low. Cover and leave on gas for a further 10minutes or until potatoes are cooked through.
- Lastly, add butter and coriander.

{Any tricky words, look in glossary.}

## Ingredients

### SERVES 4

5/6 carrots washed and sliced in the way of the carrot

2 large potatoes cut into diced into small pieces

4 pieces of garlic crushed

1small onion finely chopped

½ tin tomatoes and half the sauce

2 table spoon of oil

1 teaspoon salt

2 green chillies chopped

½ teaspoon huldi

½ teaspoon chilli powder

Dollop of butter

# PARTHA {PULPED AUBERGINE}

## Method:

- Place aubergine on the gas hob burning the skin, turn over until all skin is burnt.
- Place in a bowl of cold water; gently peel of skin, leaving only the flesh, place in a colander to drain of excess water.
- In a karai {deep frying pan} add oil fry onions on low heat until golden brown.
- Add salt, green chilli, chilli powder, tomatoes and ginger, mix well.
- Add aubergine, using a masher, mash it into the mixture mix well by turning it over covering all of the aubergine.
- As oil is releasing from the sides of the pan add masala and garnish with coriander, keep on very low heat for an extra 1min.
- Serve with hot or cold roti.

## Ingredients

### SERVES 4

2 large aubergines

2/3 large onions sliced finely

Small piece of ginger finely chopped

1 green chilli chopped

½ level teaspoon salt

½teaspoon chilli powder

Piece of fresh ginger finely chopped

2 tablespoons oil

2 /3 fresh tomatoes chopped

1level spoonful of masala

Coriander for garnish

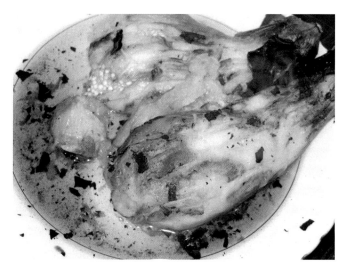

# METHI ALOO {FENUGREEK WITH POTATOES}

## Method:

- In a karai add margarine, methi and salt. Cover and leave on low heat, until soft and can easily tear away to the touch, dry up all the water that's released from methi and put to one side.
- {Tip: To dry excess water, when making methi, put methi to sides of karai, leaving the water in the centre it will quickly evaporate without burning methi}
- Next, In a chip pan fry potatoes, drain and add to methi add green chillies and chilli flakes.
- Best served with cold chapatti wraps.

{This is a good dry dish for picnics}

{Tip Less salt is safer, as you can add more after tasting it ,but if you think you've put too much in, add another potato as it will absorb extra salt. This can apply to any dish that's got more salt than needed}

{see tips pg192-194}

## Ingredients

### SERVES 4

2 /3 bunches of methi, plucked, chopped and washed

2/3 large potatoes cut into small bite size

1 level teaspoon salt

1 level spoonful of chilli flakes

2 green chillies finely chopped

1 level tablespoon of clarified  margarine.

46

# Kolma Sagg

{PUREED SPRING CABBAGE MIXED WITH SPINACH}

## Method:

- Wash each separate leaf of spring cabbage and drain in colander.
- Next, slice cabbage very thinly, put it in a deep pan and add salt, ginger, water, and margarine. Bring to boil and simmer on low heat.
- Once cabbage has wilted after about 10 minutes, add baby leaves and green chillies to pan, mix well, cover and simmer for a further half hour to 45mins.
- Cabbage should at this point be soft to touch, and easily break away, take cabbage off the heat and let it cool.
- Remove cabbage from pan add corn flour and blend it in a blender.
- Next, pour it back into pan on medium heat, and dry up the excess water.
- {Tip: With a table spoon move cabbage to sides of pan, leaving the water in the middle of the pan. This method helps dry the cabbage without burning it.
- Finally, add chilli flakes}
- Now, in a frying pan add clarified margarine and fry onions until golden brown. Add all contents of frying pan to cabbage, for extra creaminess add a large dollop of fresh butter.

Best served with maki di roti, corn flour chapatti. {See pg108}

## Ingredients

### SERVES 3/4

1 average size packet of spring cabbage

1 average size packet spinach

1 teaspoon of salt

½ pint of water

3 Green chillies finely chopped

Small piece of ginger finely chopped

Pinch of chilli flakes

Spoonful of corn flour

1 Small onion, sliced thinly

Spoonful, of clarified margarine

Dollop of butter

# DISHES MADE FROM LEFT OVER SPINACH

If you have cooked spinach left, you can turn it over and make a new dish by adding potatoes or streaky bacon.

## Method:

- In a non-stick pan add oil and onions, fry till lightly brown and soft.
- Next add potatoes {and bacon} and fry for a further minute, add green chilli, tomato, ginger and salt {do not add salt if already adding bacon}.
- Cover for 3/4 minutes until potatoes are cooked and water has evaporated.
- Finally add contents of spinach and chilli flakes.

  {Tip} You can add almost any meat to this dish ,just remember that meat needs extra time for it to cook, it also needs salt.

  {Tip} Cut meat into thin strips when adding to spinach.

## Ingredients

### SERVES 4

Left over spinach

1 medium size potato diced into small chunks
OR
4/5 streaky rinds of bacon

1 green chilli finely chopped

Small piece of ginger finely chopped

1 small onion thinly sliced

¼ teaspoon salt

1 fresh tomato diced

Large pinch of chilli flakes

1 tablespoon oil

# Kerela Alloo {Kerala with potatoes}

## Method:

- Kerela is a very bitter vegetable, if not prepared and cooked properly it could ruin the taste. It is an acquired taste.
- Using a potato peeler, peel lightly removing the bumps, slice like a cucumber, wash and drain in a colander.
- Next, in a deep frying pan fry kerelas till golden brown. Drain in a large sieve.
- Next, fry onions in the same oil until golden brown. Drain on top of the kerelas.
- In the same oil fry potato wedges until light brown and cooked through
- To the kerelas, onions and fried potatoes, add rest of the ingredients mix well.
- Next take all of the drained vegetables and transfer into a karai. Cover and leave on low heat for a further ¾ minutes until tomato softens and mixes into the dish.
- Garnish with fresh coriander, serve with hot tandoori roti {see pg110}

  {Any tricky words look in glossary}

## Ingredients

### SERVES 4

1 large kerela with the top of the kerela skin bumps, slightly peeled, top and tailed and sliced into thin slices

2 large onions finely sliced

1 large potato cut into wedges

1 fresh tomato whole

2 green chillies chopped

Small piece of fresh ginger chopped

½ teaspoon salt

½ teaspoon chilli flakes

½ of a fresh lemon in thin slices

Oil for deep frying

# Jiven Alloo {jiven potatoes}

## Method:

- Put potatoes in a bowl
- Add salt, huldi, masala, chilli flakes and green chilli
- In a blender, blend garlic, tomatoes and sauce
- Next, pour all the blended mixture over the potatoes
- Next, heat oil, add jiven ,once it has changed colour add potatoes and the rest of the mixed ingredients
- Bring to the boiling and cover with foil
- Now, lower the heat to very low for at least 15 / 20 minutes until potatoes are cooked through
- Garnish with coriander
- Best served in a roti wrap {see pg54}

{see pg54}

## Ingredients

### SERVES 4

1 tablespoon oil

2 large potatoes diced

2 pieces of garlic crushed {optional}

Large pinch of jiven

½ teaspoon salt

½ teaspoon huldi

1 green chilli chopped fine

1 teaspoon masala

½ teaspoon chilli flakes

½ tin of tomatoes and half the sauce

Fresh coriander for garnish

# Samosas

## Method:

- In a bowl put potatoes, salt, chilli powder, masala and jeera. Mash mixture, add peas and put to one side.

## Pastry Method:

- Put flour in a bowl, add margarine and rub together making sure it's all mixed.
- Now take a handful of the mixture, hold it in the palm of your hand, if it holds together, it is ready. If it won't hold, add little more margarine, and repeat holding process.
- Now, little by little, add water and gather flour making it into a ball, leave and cover for at least 1 hour.
- {Tip: Pastry can be made night before always leave it to sit in a carrier or food bag. This way it doesn't create a crust on top and make it hard to roll out.}
- Make 10 table tennis size balls, out of the pastry, roll out each ball the size of a small saucer.
- Slice in half place flat on four of your fingers on your left hand, with fingers or pastry brush put water on the top edge, making it into a cone.

- Take a spoonful of potato mix and put it into the cone.
- Next, close top of samosa with fingers, to neaten it get a fork, and press down edge.
- Heat oil, in a deep pan, test by dropping a tiny piece of pastry in it, when it rises to the top, it is hot and ready to fry.
- Now, gently put in about 4 /5 at a time, fry on medium heat turning over and fry other side bring heat up to high, drain out onto kitchen paper
- Serve with mint yogurt sauce or Imbali sauce. {See pg72 and 82 for chutney and sauces.}

## Ingredients
### MAKES 15/18

3 large potatoes, peeled and boiled

Small tin of peas

1 teaspoon salt

½ teaspoon chilli powder

½ teaspoon masala

Pinch jeera spice

### PASTRY
3 Cups of plain flour

2 spoonful of clarified margarine

1 cup of water

# Broccoli

## Method:

- In a karai or frying pan add oil and onions, fry till soft
- Next add broccoli, salt, green chillies and ginger, cover and lower to a very low heat
- Cook for 5/7 minutes till broccoli has turned soft
- Turn heat to high and dry off excess water, finally add chilli flakes

{Tip: To slice broccoli using a sharp knife cut through the middle, this makes it easier to cut of smaller pieces.}

{Best served in a cold roti wrap}

## Ingredients

### SERVES 2

1 whole broccoli washed and sliced into small pieces

2 green chillies finely chopped

Small piece of ginger sliced thinly

¼ teaspoon salt

½ teaspoon chilli flakes

Tablespoon oil

1 medium onion thinly sliced

# Sweet dishes Healthy drinks and Snacks

Achar Making {homemade pickle}

Matiaee {sugar coated bites}

Baby potatoes in Imbali sauce

Dai Pakoria {yogurt with pakoria}

Dai Pallae {yogurt with homemade dumplings}

Homemade Yoghurt

Halva

Sweet Besan

Matia {salt and black pepper biscuits}

Kava {healthy drink}

Imbali Chutney {Tamarind sweet sour sauce}

Mix Pakora

The best cup of Punjabi tea

Sewia {vermicelli}

Seera {sweet pudding made with chappati flour}

Fish Pakora

Plain Pakora

Spicy Chicken Wraps

# Achar making {homemade pickle}

## Method:

- Slice carrots into three pieces, then into strips.
- Next, peel and slice ginger into half then strips.
- Slice chillies through the middle to make two and finely slice lemons into thin pieces.
- Put all ingredients into a large bowl that will allow enough room for you to be able to mix well and coat all ingredients. Add salt, huldi chilli powder, mango pickle and oil, mix well.
- Now bottle it in a seal tight jar.
- It can be eaten right away although it's best when it has absorbed all the other flavours.

{Tip: Pickle can stay fresh in a jar for 6 months}

{Tip: Never put a wet spoon in jar as pickle will quickly go off and create a fungus on it}

## Ingredients

3/4 Carrots washed and dried

2 lemons washed and dried

6/7 Fat green chillies washed and dried

1 Large piece of ginger peeled and dried

200grms of mango pickle

1 Cup oil

Big handful salt

Big handful huldi

Teaspoon chilli powder

A glass jar for bottling pickle

# Matiaee {sugar coated bites}

## Method:

- In a bowl pour flour and margarine, mix with hand
- Next, make a dough gradually add water, you will not need all the water only use enough and bind dough together.
- Put to one side for 10 minutes to let it sit.
- Next roll out dough to ½ cm thickness, then with a sharp knife score into strips.
- Then score opposite direction, cutting into small cubes
- Next heat oil to very hot, test by dropping a bit of dough, if it rises quickly it is hot enough.
- Now gently drop a few squares at a time and fry on low heat gently turning them for 4 /5 minutes. Drain them out onto kitchen paper.
- For syrup in a pan pour 3/4 of a cup of water, add sugar and boil for 15 minutes
- Place squares in a pyrex bowl and gently pour syrup over them coating them.

  {Tip: Do a few at a time to evenly coat them, but be quick as the syrup will dry quickly}

  Best served hot with a cup of Punjabi Tea!

## Ingredients

1 ½ cups of self rising flour

1 spoonful of clarified margarine

3 cups of sugar

1 cup of water

{Tip: Double the sugar to the flour}

# Baby potatoes in imbali sauce

## Method:

- Place Imbali in a jug and pour boiling water on it
- Leave Imbali in for half hour until it gets soft, and breaks away
- Next place potatoes in a pan with water add salt and butter boil till cooked through
- Drain potatoes and slice thinly and spread them onto serving plate
- Sprinkle masala and chilli powder
- Sieve the Imabli sauce into serving jug press over the Imbali and squeeze as much out and pour over the potatoes.
- A very sweet and sour dish a treat on hot days .

## Ingredients

### 2 SERVINGS

Small bag of baby potatoes roughly about 10 for each serving

Teaspoon butter

Salt to taste

Pinch chilli powder

Pinch masala

½ a block of Imbali

1 pint of boiling water

# DAI PAKORIA {YOGURT WITH PAKORIA}

## Method:

- In a bowl pour yogurt
- Next add pakoria, green chillies, milk, masala and salt and stir lightly.
- Finish off with coriander, simple as that.

{Tip: Dai pakoria is best served chilled}

{Tip: If you think dai pakoria is too thick add a little more chilled milk}

{Tip: If you want to serve them straight away, put pakoria in a bowl of warm water to soften them. Squeeze them out and add to yogurt}

## Ingredients

1 medium tub of yogurt

½ cup of chilled milk

2 green chillies finely chopped

Handful fresh chopped coriander

½ cups of pakoria

Pinch of salt

Pinch masala

# Dai pallai
{YOGURT WITH HOMEMADE DUMPLINGS}

## Method:

- Pour urid daal flour into a bowl add ½ teaspoon baking powder, gradually add water and mix.
- Keep mixing until you have a batter consistency.
- Leave to sit for at least one hour
- Heat oil and drop a few spoonfuls at a time and fry, let the mixture rise, then lower heat and let dumplings cook through.
- Next, put heat up to high, and cook for a further couple of minutes. Drain on kitchen paper and put aside to cool.
- In a bowl pour in yogurt add green chillies, spring onions, jeera, masala and salt.
- Next, put dai pallai in warm water, squeeze them out before adding to yogurt.
- Gently stir making sure all dumplings are immersed, let them sit for 4-5 minutes in the fridge before serving.

{Tip: If yogurt looks too thick add chilled milk.}

## Ingredients

300 gram of urid daal powder

Oil for frying

Medium tub of yogurt

½teaspoon of baking powder

Salt to taste {about ½ teaspoon}

Pinch masala

Pinch jeera

2/3 spring onions finely chopped

2 green chillies finely chopped

½ cup of chilled milk

# HOMEMADE YOGURT

## Method:

- Pour milk in a deep pan and bring to boil
- Let it cool down to luke warm, gently stir in the yogurt pot, and cover with foil leave in a warm place in the kitchen overnight.
- Once yogurt has set it can be put into pots and kept in fridge for a couple of days.

## Mint yogurt

- In a bowl put to 3/4 tablespoons of home made yogurt add teaspoon of mint sauce, pinch of masala and pinch of salt, and pinch of jeera.
- Chill in fridge for 1 hour, before serving with samosas and pakoras.

## Mint chutney

- You will need a mortar and pestle, alternatively you can use a food processor.
- Take all ingredients and blend using either method
- Lastly add salt, cool in fridge for half hour before serving.
- This chutney is best when served with daals and rice.

## Ingredients

### MINT YOGHURT
Small pot of yogurt

2/3 pints of full cream, or sterilised milk


### MINT CHUTNEY
5 /6 fresh mint leaves

1 large onion

1 green chilli

1 small piece of ginger

Handful fresh coriander

Pinch of salt

Pinch of imbali

# Halva

## Method:

- In a pan, put water and ¾ of the sugar, let it dissolve on low heat, once it is dissolved take it off the heat.
- In another pan and on very low heat add semolina and flour.
- Now gradually add some of the butter, making sure all semolina is coated. If mixture looks a little dry then add a bit more butter and keep on sifting it back and forth with a tablespoon until it changes colour slightly and butter is released at the edges of the pan. Also at this stage you will be able to smell the aroma.
- Keeping the pan on the gas slowly add the sugar water stirring all the time as halva thickens to a consistency of a pudding {you don't need to add all the sugar water}
- Next add cardomn seeds and the extra sugar stirring all through the process.
- Finish halva by sprinkling almonds.

  {Tip: When adding sugar water keep pan facing away from your face as it starts to bubble and spit.}

## Ingredients

1 small cup of semolina

1 large pinch of self rising flour

250grm of clarified unsalted butter

2 cups of sugar

Large pinch of flaked almonds

5/6 small cardomn seeds

1 pint of water

# Sweet Besan

{Sweet dish made from gramflour with pistachios and almonds}

## Method:

- In a karai, pour in besan then slowly add butter covering all the besan. Add semolina and keep karai on very low heat. Slowly sift the besan back and forth.
- This method is helping fry the besan slowly and it will take about 15/ 20 minutes. You will now be at the point where the besan is creating soft bubbles and you will be able to see butter from the sides of the karai.
- It should now look like golden sand, turn down heat add sugar and mix by sifting back and forth.
- Now sprinkle pistachios and almonds.

{Tip: Once cooled down; besan can be poured into small containers and kept for 4 weeks in a fridge, taken out in small quantities and heated in a microwave for a few seconds or until it's warmed to your liking}

Or you can pour it straight into a baking tray, and once cooled down score it into squares.

Cold besan is comforting on cold nights, with a hot Punjabi cup of tea.

## Ingredients

2 cups besan

1 1b of unsalted clarified butter

¼ cup of semolina

½ cup of crushed pistachios

½ cup of crushed almonds

2 1b of sugar

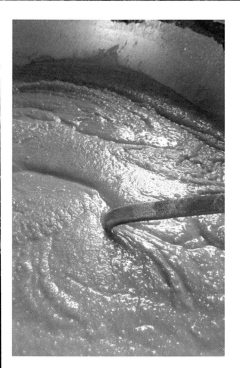

# Matia

## {SALT AND BLACK PEPPER BISCUITS}

## Method:

- In a bowl add flour, salt, black pepper and margarine, use your hands mix well - like pastry.

- Now take a small amount of flour mix from the bowl and squeeze it in the palm of your hand, it should bind together, now hold the piece and break it into two, at this point if it breaks off neatly, this means there is enough margarine in the pastry.

- Slowly add water little by little with left hand and gather flour with right hand keeping it almost dry like.

- Gently knead it a couple of times and with your hands roll out a long sausage like dough, and with a knife cut out equal pieces.

- Take each piece and flatten it with your hand, just needs one hard press with your palm, now roll it out. It should be smaller than a saucer, and very thin, take a fork and poke to release the air bubbles.

- Matia, when rolled doesn't have to be neat at the edge, that's what makes a mati {salt and black pepper biscuit} different. Although you can roll pastry, and cut out biscuits, fry in the same way.

- Next, heat oil in karai or deep frying pan, drop a tiny ball of dough and once it rises to the top quickly, oil is hot enough. Gently place a few matia at a time and fry, and keep turning them so that they are equally fried to a golden brown.

- Once fried, drain onto kitchen paper, frying, should take no longer than 30 seconds, each side or until matia are light golden brown.

- To make the fingers, each individual rolled out mati needs to be cut like strips and fried exactly the same.

- Matia can be fried straight away, or dough can be put it the fridge for later frying for when guests are arriving. Matia has a different taste when they are freshly out of the frying pan{karai} and a different taste when the are cold.

- You can also heat matia in the microwave, wrap one matia at a time in kitchen paper, heat it for 20 seconds, let it cool and you will have a crisp hot mati.

## Ingredients
### 14/15 biscuits or fingers

2 ½ cups of plain flour

1 Dessert spoon of clarified margarine

Fair pinch of salt

Double fair pinch of freshly ground black pepper

1 drinking glass of water, although you won't need all of it

Oil for frying

{Tip: When frying matia, always make sure it is fresh clean oil, or oil which has just been used for matia only}

# Kava {HEALTHY DRINK}

A healthy drink, when appetite is low, or when you've just had an upset stomach and can't keep any food down.

## Method:

- Pour water into saucepan, add all ingredients and bring to boil.
- Simmer on low heat until all of the liquid has condensed to about 1 cup.
- Now sieve into a cup or glass and drink, whilst still warm.

    This recipe is centuries old and still the best Punjabi drink to help recover quickly and bring back your appetite.

## Ingredients

1 pint water

2 peppercorns

1 big lachi {black cardomn}

2 /3 mint leaves

Pinch of salt

Small piece of ginger {optional}

# Imbali Chutney
{Tamarind sweet sour sauce}

## Method:

- In a bowl or jug add water and imabli, let it dissolve by stirring it until it is all loose.
- Next seive into a bowl, press imbali so all the flavour goes into bowl
- Next add salt, sugar, lemon, chilli powder and carrots
- Mix well, pour into a jug and let it cool in fridge for at least an hour before serving
- Best served with samosa

## Ingredients

1 small block of Imbali

1 pint boiling hot water

1 teaspoon sugar

½ teaspoon salt

Pinch of chilli powder

Squeeze of half a lemon

½ Carrot shredded finely

# Mix Pakora

## Method:

- Into a bowl put potatoes, aubergine, coriander, onions, spring leaves, salt, chilli powder and green chillies.
- Next add a tablespoon of gram flour, mix well gradually adding a little more gram flour until all ingredients are covered.
- Next add a spoonful of oil, mix with table spoon and leave the mixture for and hour, to release water from the onions.
- {Tip: Only add a little water if in a hurry to fry}
- Now heat oil to very hot, test by dropping a tiny bit of the mixture, once it quickly rises to the top, it is hot enough.
- Next with a spoon gently lower 6 or 7 spoonfuls of mixture in the oil, once the pakora rises lower the heat to let ingredients cook through, this should be about a minute. Now put the heat back up to full, and turn over pakoras equally until crispy.
- Drain onto kitchen paper. Serve hot

   {Tip: By adding greens, of any kind gives the pakora, the crispiness. Greens you could use are methi leaves, flat lettuce and cauliflower leaves or coriander}

   Try spinach pakoras. Thin sliced onions, small bag of baby spinach and a small dice potato.

## Ingredients

3 large onions sliced thin

1 ½ cups of gram flour or 3 /4 tablespoon

1 large potato, cut into small thin pieces

½ aubergine cut into small thin pieces

1 green chilli chopped

½ bag of baby spinach leaves

1 teaspoon salt

1 teaspoon chilli powder

Handful coriander chopped

1 spoonful oil

Oil for deep frying

# THE BEST CUP OF PUNJABI TEA

## Method:

- In a saucepan add 5cups of water, add teabags.
- Lachi, peppercorns and sugar {optional} bring to boil and simmer for 1 minute.
- Now, add milk to taste and boil for further 1/2 mins on low heat.
- Sieve and serve.

  {Tip: You can use ginger or cinnamon stick instead of peppercorns to give that extra kick.}

  {Tip: You can use fresh mint leaves instead of cardomn to give a refreshing taste.}

  {Tip: By boiling the tea for additional minutes it gives it a rich taste of brewed tea. Tea can also be made with only milk instead of water}

## Ingredients
### 3/4 CUPS

2 tea bags

1 small lachi {cardomn}

2 black peppercorns

Milk to taste

Sugar to taste

# SEWIA {VERMICELLI}

## Method:

- Break sewia into a pan; roast them by tossing them over every few minutes and not allowing them to stick to the pan.
- {Tip: Hold handle, lift pan and turn them over shaking pan, repeating process}
- Alternatively use tablespoon to turn them around, so that all sewia are roasted.
- Once roasted put them aside.
- In a deep pan put water to boil about ¾ full.
- Once it comes to boiling point gently add sewia, boil them for 10/12 mins, to test if they are cooked take one and press it with your finger and thumb, it should break off quickly
- Drain sewia into a colander.
- For each serving put few spoonfuls into cereal bowl add teaspoon of butter and spoonful of sugar mix well.

  {Tip: Sewia can be cooked the night before, cooled and left in fridge. Just remember to add sugar and butter after heating in microwave just before serving}

## Ingredients

### 5/6 SERVINGS

¾pkt of sewia

Sugar to taste

Teaspoon of butter for each individual serving

# SEERA {SWEET PUDDING MADE WITH CHAPATTI FLOUR}

## Method:

- Put flour, into a wide frying pan and on low heat with a table spoon sift it back and forth evenly around, this method is cooking the flour at the same time, browning it without burning it.
- This will take 5/6 minutes, at this stage the flour will change colour to a golden brown.
- Next, sieve flour, removing any lumps and put to one side.
- In a deep pan pour water and sugar keeping it on medium heat, once sugar has dissolved, slowly sprinkle all of the flour, using a hand whisk ,mix it until all the flour has blended with the sugar water.
- Now, increase the heat and keep stirring until mixture thickens to a creamy consistency, finally add butter to taste.
- Extra butter can be added to individual servings.

{Best served on cold nights or as a pick me up after a lost appetite.}

{Tip: If you find it difficult to remove lumps, pour all of the mixture into a blender and then, back into a pan and cook as normal.}

## Ingredients
### 5/6 SERVINGS

1 cup chapatti flour

½ lb of sugar

2 pints water

Thin slice of butter {roughly 1 inch}

90

# FISH PAKORA

## Method:

- Slice cod into 1 inch pieces; wash with cold water and drain.
  {Tip: Make sure fish has drained for at least half hour, because it will affect the way the fish will fry}
- Next place fish pieces onto tray and sprinkle lemon juice.
- Take a large pinch of salt and rub equally onto fish.
- Take large pinch of chilli powder and rub equally onto fish.
- Next take a handful of flour and sparingly cover fish and put to one side.
- In a bowl, put flour and big pinch of huldi. Slowly add water, and mix with a whisk.
- You should now have a batter consistency.
- Next, add eggs and whisk until smooth.
- Leave batter to sit, for at least 30 minutes, although, if in a hurry, you could fry it straight away.
  {Tip: You can put these ingredients into a blender to make it easy!}
- Heat oil, test by dropping some batter, and if it rises quickly to top then the oil is hot enough.
- Next dip the fish into batter and then straight into pan, let it rise to the top and once the batter has set onto fish lower the heat for a minute and let fish cook through.
- Now bring heat up to very high, once it looks golden brown and crisp drain it onto kitchen paper.
- Best served with crispy homemade chips. Yummie!

## Ingredients
### 5/6 SERVINGS

1 packet of cod cut

2cups of selfrizing flour

2 eggs

Drizzle of lemon juice

Salt large pinch

Chilli powder large pinch

Pinch of huldi powder

Handful of selfrising flour

# Plain Pakora

## Method:

- In a bowl put gram flour, salt, chilli powder, masala, jeera and coriander.
- Next, gradually add water and mix with a whisk to make batter.
  {Tip: You can save time and put all in a blender}
- Heat oil to very hot, and then bring it to very low.
- Next, dip potato and aubergine alternatively into batter and gently drop into oil.
- Bring heat up to high and fry pakora for a few seconds or until it looks like the batter has set onto the pakora.
- Now lower the heat again and let the pakora cook through for a further minute.
- Turn heat to very high, letting the pakora crisp up, drain on kitchen paper.

  Serve as a side dish with any daal or on its own, with a freshly buttered roti.
  {MOUTH WATERING}

## Ingredients
### MAKES 10/12

1 large potato peeled and sliced whole

1 aubergine sliced thinly; keep slices round by following the shape of the aubergine

3/4 tablespoons of gram flour

1 teaspoon salt

1 level spoonful of chilli powder

Pinch of masala

Pinch of jeera

Large handful of chopped coriander

Water for mixing

Oil for frying

94

# Spicy chicken wraps

## Method:

- Place oil in pan, keep heat medium, add onions and fry till lightly brown
- Next add chicken, turn over gently, add salt, chilliflakes, green chilli. Gently turn over mixing all ingredients
- Add tomatoes and peppers, gently turn over, cover and lower heat to let meat cook through
- After about 5/6 minutes check to see if meat is cooked, if oil is releasing from the sides of the pan it is ready
- Finally add masala and garnish with coriander.
- Once you have made wrap you may wish to spread a very thin layer of butter {optional}
- Place wrap on a clean surface, dry side down, put a layer of lettuce and cucumber
- Next place 2 pieces on top of lettuce, now fold from the bottom and then wrap over right, then left.

## Ingredients

### MAKES 2

4 chicken mini fillets

Tablespoon oil

1 green chilli cut in half

2 small onions thinly sliced

1 tablespoon of tinned tomatoes

½ a large green pepper thinly sliced

¼ teaspoon salt

¼ teaspoon chilli flakes

Large pinch of masala

Spoonful butter

Coriander to garnish

3 pieces thinly sliced cucumber

Iceberg lettuce

2 wraps
{see how to make a roti }
Just make the ball little bigger than a normal roti and roll it out bigger than usual size.

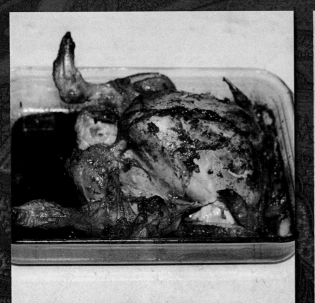

Jeera

5 mix masala

Chilli powder

Salt

chilli flakes

Tumeric

Jiven

# Breads

Roti {Chappati}

Misi Roti

Maki di roti {corn flour chapattis}

Tandoori Roti

Suchia {large fried plain flour bread}

Puri {small fried bread}

Plain Prantha

Alloo Stuffed Parantha

Paturae {small fried naan bread}

# ROTI {CHAPPATI}

## Ingredients
### 5/6 ROTI

3/ 4 cups of chapatti flour

1 pint of water

## Method: making the dough

- Pour flour into a bowl
- Gradually add some water with left hand and gather with right hand, you will not need all the water only use enough to make a dough.
- Knead it couple of times and then fold it over, leave for at least half hour for the dough to sit. It can be rolled straight away but his makes it easier to roll.

## Method:

- Heat Tava to very hot, and then lower the heat.
- Rub the heated tava with a tea towel.
- Make equal size balls from the dough and with a firm hand press the ball.
- Next place your thumb in the middle of the ball and keep pressing around the edges turning clockwise at the same time. {This method of flattening makes it easy when you roll a roti.}
- Now with a rolling pin, roll out to a little bigger than a side plate size.
- Lift roti and place onto left hand with a firm slap, place it onto right hand repeat left to right a couple of times, this makes the roti expand a little more.
- Place roti, onto heated tava, once it starts to change colour, turn roti over, let this side cook completely.
- Now, turn roti back onto 1st side and with a clean tea towel press and at the same time keep turning it clockwise. This should take only a few seconds.
- Lastly, with spoon butter the side that's been pressed.
- Try sugar and butter roll.
- Take a freshly made roti, spread a generous amount of butter, then a thin layer of sugar, roll up roti and have a taste. YUMMIE! Or simply eat dry!

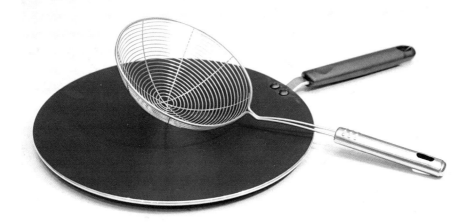

Flattened ball

Dough balls

Dough

# Misi Roti

## Method:

- In a bowl pour flour and gram flour, mix with hand and add salt, chilli powder, green chillies, onion, coriander, and anar dana.
- Next, mix all ingredients and make a well, gradually add water and by rolling it around in the bowl creat a ball of dough. Knead it a couple of times and leave dough in the bowl, giving it time to rest.
- Once dough has rested for at least 1 hour it can be rolled and cooked.
- Make one small tennis size ball and roll it to a saucer size.
- Next, lift the roti and place it on your left palm, by gently slapping roti onto right palm and then repeating process a couple of times lets the roti expand to a size just little smaller than a round dinner plate size, which of course is the correct size.
- Heat tava, place roti on tava, as roti starts to cook it will change colour. Turn onto other side, cook this side more.
- Once it's fully cooked, turn over onto 1st side pressing it down with a clean tea towel and turning it round clockwise at the same time.
- Once cooked pinch roti in a few places and spread butter on the pinched side, serve with plain yogurt and achar.
- The reason for pinching the roti, gives it texture and so butter melts in the dips keeping it generously moist.

{Can be served hot or cold. Great for picnics}

## Ingredients
### 8/10 ROTI

4 cups chapatti flour

3 cups of gram flour

Fair pinch of salt

Handful coriander chopped

2 green chillies finely chopped

Fair pinch of chilli powder

1 large onion minced

Large pinch of dried pomegranate seeds (anar dana) this is optional

1 ½ pints of cold water

{You will not need all the water ,only use enough to make dough}

Butter

Flattened ball

Dough balls

Dough

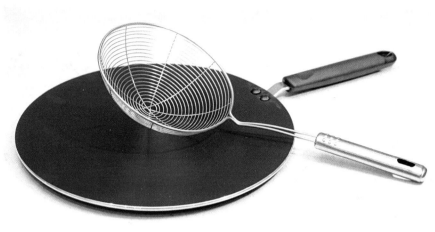

# MAKI DI ROTI {CORN FLOUR CHAPATTIS}

## Method:

- In a bowl pour one quarter of the corn flour and 1 spoonful of chapatti flour.
- Gradually add boiling water, at the same time use a tablespoon and mix.
- Once mixed, make a ball and then flatten it with the palm of your hand, lightly dip it in plain flour, this will help when rolling and not stick to bag.
- Now heat tava to very hot, and then lower the heat, now wipe tava with a little butter or oil.
  {Tip: Wiping the tava with butter or oil prevents makai roti from sticking}
- Take the flattened dough and place it between a food bag. If you don't have a food bag alternatively you can use a clean carrier bag.
- Using a rolling pin gently roll it slightly smaller than a normal roti.
- Next, slit the bag from the top and place your right hand on top of rolled out roti. With your left hand lift from underneath the bag with a firm lift place roti on your right hand and then straight onto tava.
- Once one side has cooked, take a spatula and lift roti and cook on other side.
- Once roti has changed colour, turn back onto the first side and press down with a clean tea towel, with gentle pressing you are cooking it through.
- Now, take roti and pinch it on the pressed side in a few places.
- Take a generous amount of butter and spread on the same side.
- The reason for pinching is to create little pockets where the dollops of butter can sit and moisturise the roti, keeping it soft.
- Alternatively you can preheat oven on grill setting, and after turning roti over once you can place it in the oven for few minutes or until it cooked.
- Best served, with kolma sagg {see pg48}

## Ingredients
## 8/10 ROTI

1 small packet 300g corn flour

Chapatti flour 4 spoonful

Boiling water

Large food bags

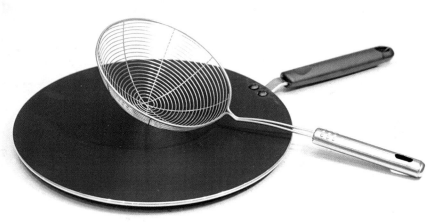

# Tandoori roti

## Method:

- In a bowl pour chapatti flour.
- Next, gradually pour water with left hand and gather flour with right hand, creating the dough. You will not need all the water only use enough to make the dough.
- Once gathered into a ball knead it a couple of times and then allow it to sit. {Tip: Letting dough sit for at least half hour, will make it easier to roll.}
- Heat tava, and at the same time put oven on grill setting.
- Make equal size balls, take one ball and with the palm of your hand, press in the middle, now place your thumb in the middle of the ball at the same time keep pressing the edges turning clockwise {This process makes it easier to roll the roti.}
- Roll roti a little bigger than a side plate, lift and place roti on left palm of your hand, then with a firm slap place it onto your right palm repeat a couple off times This process helps expand the roti, it should be done very quickly, and reason for this is for the roti not to shrink back.
- Lift roti and place on tava cook side fully, now lift roti and place cooked side down, with a pastry brush wet uncooked side with water making sure all that side of the roti is wet.
- Place roti under the grill wet side facing grill, cook for a few seconds or until fully cooked.
- Spread butter on grilled side; serve with any fresh vegetable dish.

  {Tip: When in a rush cook roti beforehand on tava, ready to be put under grill}

## Ingredients

3 cups of chapatti flour

1 pint of water

# SUCHIA {LARGE FRIED PLAIN FLOUR BREAD}

## Ingredients
### MAKES 5/6

5/6 cups of plain flour

Pinch of salt

Luke warm water

Oil for frying

## Method:

- Pour flour into a bowl and add salt. Make a well and gradually add little water with left hand and gather flour with right hand, making a ball as your hand works round.

- Now knead it a couple of times and pour spoonful of oil on dough, let dough sit for at least and hour before cooking.
{Tip: The longer the dough sits, the easier it is to roll.}

- Now, make 5/6 equal tennis size balls and put a drop of oil on them.

- In a karai {deep frying pan} add oil enough for deep frying, heat it, and test by dropping a tiny ball in the oil. Once it rises up to the surface quickly, that means it is hot enough.

- Now, lower the heat, take one ball and roll it to a saucer size.

- Next, lift it and dip it lightly into a plate of dry flour, put it back on worktop and roll a little more to the size of a dinner plate.

- Lift it off the worktop and lay it flat on the palm of your left hand and with your right hand pull equally all round slowly stretching the dough.

- It should be now bigger than a dinner plate, gently hold it from the top and carefully place it in oil, and put the heat up to full.

- When the dough touches the hot oil, it will cook very quickly, so have a spatula ready to turn suchi over to other side, it only takes about a minute for a suchi to fry.

- {Tip: A round spatula with tiny holes is the perfect utensil, for frying bread. See utensil picture pg14-15 }

- Drain onto kitchen paper. Suchia can be eaten hot or cold with chick peas.

- {A suchi tastes delicious the following day. Heat it on a tava. As it heats it begins to add extra crispiness, beat 2/3 eggs with pinch of salt, pinch of masala, pinch of chilli powder and coriander. Heat spoonful of clarified margarine and gently fold in egg}

{Any tricky words see glossary}

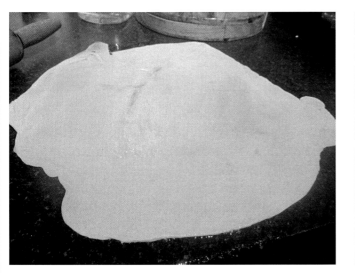

# PURI {SMALL FRIED BREAD}

## Method:

- Pour flour into a deep bowl, make a well and slowly add little water, bringing the flour together. It should be almost like it's dry.
- Once you've gathered it all, take tablespoon of oil and pour over dough. Then knead it a few times, spreading oil over the partly dry dough.
- The dough should now be together, and feel a little firmer than when making a chapatti.
- Put dough into a carrier or food bag, and let it settle for at least 20minutes in the fridge
- {Tip: Letting dough sit for at least 20 minutes makes puris roll out smooth although if in a rush, it can be rolled and fried straight away.
- Take dough out of fridge and make 8/10 equal size balls, use extra oil on hands to stop the balls from sticking.
- Next, roll out each ball to the size of a small saucer and place in an oil lined tray. By laying them in a tray with a lining of oil it stops the puris from sticking.
- In a karai, heat oil for deep frying {deep frying pan} test if oil is hot enough, by dropping a tiny bit of the dough into the hot oil, if it rises to the top very quickly it is ready.
- Now, lift one puri at a time and gently lower into oil carefully, lower the heat. Take a spatula with holes and turn over and fry other side this should be done quickly, roughly 30 seconds each side.
- Drain onto kitchen paper.

## Ingredients
### MAKES 8/10

4/5 cups of chapatti flour

Jug of water

Tablespoon oil

Oil for frying

# Plain prantha

## Method:

- Make dough see pg104 for roti and let it sit for at least 1 hour
- This will make the dough easy to roll
- Next make equal size balls, double the size of when making a roti.
- Next take one ball and press it flat, sprinkle pinch of salt evenly and spread spoonful of clarified margarine
- Next fold it over and then roll it like a sausage, once in sausage form, curl it like a catherine wheel
- Next place flat and roll out to a dinner plate size
- Heat tava, lift prantha and gently place it onto tava
- Lower heat to medium and let side cook, lift prantha and cook other side, gently spread oil.
- Fry till golden brown and crisp, turn back to 1st side and repeat, dry off onto kitchen paper.
- Serve with any daal or scrambled egg or any veg dish with achar.
- Plain prantha can be eaten on its own.

## Ingredients
### MAKES 2/3

3 / 4 cups of chapatti flour

2 Tablespoon of clarified margarine

Oil for frying

Pinch of salt

Water

# ALLOO STUFFED PRATHA

## Method:

- Make dough see pg104 for roti and let it sit for at least 1 hour
- In a bowl, mash potatoes, add salt, green chillies, onion, chilli powder, and coriander mix well.
- Next, take the dough roll 2 balls slightly bigger than a when making a roti.
- Next, flatten them out, to a size, slightly smaller than a saucer, now take a small amount of the mixture and place it in the middle, patting it evenly, then place the other one on top and close it by pressing all round the sides making sure there is no air trapped, use dry flour to help you roll it.
- {Tip: Once you place the other part of the dough on top, start by gently pressing from the middle as this will prevent air bubbles, and not tear whilst rolling it out.}
- Next, lightly roll it out to a dinner plate size.
- Heat tava and lift prantha by placing it on your left palm, then flip it quickly onto tava.
- Cook one side until colour changes, turn over to other side, with spoon, spread oil or clarified margarine to fry prantha repeat on other side once fried, dry off on kitchen paper, serve with achar.

  {Any tricky words look in glossary}

## Ingredients

### MAKES 4

2 large potatoes boiled and mashed

1 small onion finely diced

1 green chilli finely chopped

1 level teaspoon salt

½ teaspoon chilli powder

½ teaspoon masala

Generous pinch of fresh coriander

### DOUGH

4/5 cups of Chappati flour to make dough

Oil or clarified margarine for frying

# Paturae {small fried naan bread}

## Method:

- In a bowl pour in flour, add jeera, coriander and mix with hands.
- Next, take the milk and water mix and slowly add a little at a time to flour, hold the bowl with the left hand and gather flour with right hand, all the time rolling and gathering into a ball, only use enough milk water mix as all will not be needed.
- Fold dough, a couple of times, pour tablespoon oil and fold again.
- Next, put dough into a carrier or food bag to rise, leave in fridge for at least an hour. Heat oil in karai {deep frying pan} To test if oil is hot enough drop a tiny bit of dough, if it rises quickly, it is ready.
- Next, lower heat, put a spoonful of oil on your palms and make equal table tennis size balls.
- Next, roll each ball to the size little bigger than a saucer.
- Lift naan, gently lower it into karai, after a couple of seconds or when you see that one side is cooked, turn over to other side, drain onto kitchen paper.
- Paturae can be eaten hot or cold.
- {Tip: When heating paturae in microwave wrap in tea towel or kitchen paper and heat for few seconds only,if heated for too long they will instantly go hard.}

  {You can roll a few at a time, and place them in a tray with a thin layer of oil to prevent them sticking, or you can roll one fry one. With practice and experience you will be able to fry a few at a time.}

## Ingredients
### MAKES 8/10

5 cups of self-rising flour

Pinch of jeera seeds (cumin seeds)

Handful of chopped coriander

¼ pint of cold milk topped up with cold water

1 table spoon oil

Oil for deep frying

# DAALS {PULSES}

## Daals are a must in the Punjabi household.

A great treat on cold days, super for vegetarians, or just a side dish complimenting the main course or snacks. {Pakoras, wara, karai, chicken} Daals can also be served on their own.

There are many kinds of pulses, but the main ones used in the average household are:

- Lentils {which is the quickest to cook 40-50minutes}
- Mava did daal {black pulses} which is great and is even tastier the next day eaten cold with a prantha a fried {flatbread} and achar {pickle}.
- This daal needs to be cooking for at least 3/4 hours on low heat, or pressure cooker.
- In mava di daal if you add a handful of ronghi {kidney beans} it cooks quicker and taste delicious.
- Rajma {kidney beans} this pulse also takes at least 3 hours, best served with plain boiled rice.
- Moong daal is best for kichree, which is a dish made with moong daal and rice.
- Chana daal is best made with marrow {kudu and dal}

# Daals

Lentils

Channa Daal with Kadu {daal with marrow}

Daal Saag {moong daal with spinach}

Mava di Daal {black daal}

Ronghi {kidney beans cooked like daal}

# Lentils

## Method:

- Wash lentils until water is clear, add all ingredients except butter, coriander and masala.
- Stir well, bring to boil and simmer on low heat for 45/50 mins checking regularly topping up with a little more water if needed.
- {Tip: Cover half the pan allowing the steam to escape as lentils boils over very quickly.}
- Once all water has evaporated and lentils has thickened to a soup like consistency add butter and coriander.
- Lentils dahl can be served on its own, or as a side dish with pakoras or best of all with plain rice, small fried potatoes like crisps, mint, ginger and imbali chutney.
- {Tarka, is optional as this gives it a more creamy texture.}
- In a frying pan add fair pinch of jeera spice, 1 spoonful oil, once roasted add contents of frying pan to daal.

## Ingredients
### SERVES 4

2 Cups of lentils

2 and half pints of water

1 level teaspoon salt

1 small onion chopped

1 teaspoon chilly flakes

½teaspoon of huldi

Spoonful clarified margarine

1 spoonful of masala

Small piece of ginger chopped

1 green chilli chopped

1 small fresh tomato chopped

Dollop of butter

Coriander

# Chania Daal with Kadu
## {Chana Daal with marrow}

## Method:

- Wash, rinse daal a few times and pour into a deep saucepan
- Next add salt chilli, flakes, ginger, tomato, huldi, green chillies spoonful clarified margarine and 2 pints of water
- Next bring to boil and let it simmer.
- Next, peel kadu {marrow} and dice it into small pieces, after rinsing it, add it to the daal stir well and let it cook on low heat for at least 45 minutes
- At this stage daal should have thickened, use the back of a tablespoon and press against the sides of the pan and blend it a little, add more water if it looks less or if it looks too thick.
- It should now look creamy add masala and coriander and remove from heat.
- In a frying pan add 2/3 pieces of crushed garlic and a spoonful of butter or margarine, once garlic has browned a little, add it to the daal, gently empty contents of frying pan, into daal.
- {This process is call Tarka and is optional, it gives the daal extra richness}
- Serve with plain prantha {flat fried bread} and achar {mango pickle}
- This daal is great served hot, but equally fabulous when served cold with a prantha and home made pickle {see pg116 & 62}

## Ingredients
## Serves 4

2 cups of daal

1 teaspoon salt

½ teaspoon chilli flakes

½ teaspoon huldi

Spoonful clarified margarine

2green chillies finely chopped

1 teaspoon masala

1 small Kadu {marrow} peeled and diced

1 Fresh tomato diced

Thin strips of freshly sliced ginger

2/3 pints of water

# DAAL SAGG {MOONG DAAL WITH SPINACH}

## Method:

- Put daal into a pan add water and rub gently breaking up any unseen dirt, pour out water from the side of the pan, then repeat a few times till water runs clear.
- Next add salt, chilli flakes, green chilli, ginger, huldi, tomato, butter and spinach.
- Now add water bring to boil and lower heat to very low and cook for 30/40 minutes.
- Next take tablespoon and stir well pressing daal to the sides of the pan smoothing and blending sagg and daal. If water seems to have dried up add little more keeping the daal to a thick soup like consistency.
- Lastly add butter and garnish with coriander.
- Serve with cold roti's and achar.
- Tarka is optional.

## Ingredients
### SERVES 4

1 cup of moong daal

½teaspoon salt

½teaspoon chilli flakes

1 green chilli chopped

1 fresh tomato

½ teaspoon huldi

Small piece of ginger chopped

1 teaspoon butter or clarified margarine

Small packet of washed spinach leaves

1pint of water

# Mava di daal

## black daal {pulse}

## Method:

- Pour daal into a large tray and pick out any stones or sticks you may find.
- It is important to do this because mava di daal {black daal} as this is the one with most bits in the packaging.
- Next put daal and kidney beans into a deep pan as this daal takes a few hours to cook.
- {Tip: When cooking this daal or kidney beans it is best to use a heavy bottom pan.}
- Now half fill pan with water, with your hands rub the daal as this will remove any bits of dried soil, which is something the naked eye can't see, so this process of washing it a few times is a must. Rub, wash and rinse do this at least 4-5 times.
- After washing daal, fill pan to the top just leaving about and inch, add all ingredients except masala and bring to boil.
- Now cover with foil and lower the heat to the lowest and let it cook for 2/3 hours, check it after an hour and then every half hour.
- At this stage it should have thickened, get the ladle and gently stir blending it by pressing it against the sides of the pan this will help it to get smooth.
- Lastly add masala and coriander.
- Tarka is optional although it helps and adds extra flavour and creaminess.
- For Tarka in a frying pan roast large pinch of jeera once they are roasted add spoonful of butter, now pour all contents into daal.
- Daal is best complimented with plain boiled rice served with fried potatoes and mint chutney.

## Ingredients
### Serves 4

3 cups of daal

1 handful kidney beans

1 level teaspoon  of salt

½ teaspoon chilli powder

Small piece of chopped ginger

1 green chilli finely chopped

1 fresh tomato chopped

1 medium size onion chopped roughly

1 spoonful oil or clarified margarine

1 spoonful of masala

Dollop of butter

Jeera for tarka  {optional}

# Ronghi {kidney beans in curry sauce}

## Method:

- Pour ronghi into a deep heavy bottom pan
- Next wash ronghi, add water ¾ into pan gently rub beans and pour out water, repeat a couple of times until water is clear.
- Next fill pan leaving about and inch from the top, bring to boil and cover with foil, let ronghi cook for at least 2/3 hours until very soft. It might take a little longer depending on the beans, let this sit for an hour.
- Now in a separate pan, add oil, onions and fry until soft add garlic until caramelised add tomatoes. Next add salt, green chilli, huldi, ginger and chilli powder, poon mixture until oil is releasing from side of the pan, add 1 cup of water and teaspoon of butter.
- Next pour mixture into boiled pan of ronghi stir well add 1 pint of water, bring to boil and let it simmer for a further 30/40 minutes until creamy.
- Lastly add dollop of butter and coriander.
- Serve with plain boiled rice and small fried potatoes.

{Tip: Ronghi tastes even better cold with a prantha - flat fried bread}

{Any tricky words look in glossary}

## Ingredients
## Serves 4

3 cups of ronghi
{or tinned kideny beans}

½ teaspoon salt

1 green chilli chopped

2 tomatoes and sauce from tin

½ teaspoon huldi

½ teaspoon chilli powder

Small piece of chopped ginger

2 tablespoons of oil

1 finely chopped onion

4/5 pieces of crushed garlic

1 teaspoon butter

Extra dollop of butter

Coriander for garnish

# Rice dishes

Perfect Plain Boiled Rice

Kichree

Karri and Chaul {karri and rice dish}

Vegetarian Pilaue {with peas or mixed veg}

Chicken Pilaue

Mitae Chaul {sweet rice}

Keer {rice pudding with pistachio}

# Perfect plain boiled rice

## Method:

- Pour rice into the pan you are using for boiling, add some water and wash rice gently rubbing it, tip out water and repeat process a couple of times.
- By doing this  you are getting rid of the starch that makes rice sticky.
- Next, in the pan add water, fill it roughly ¾ and bring to boil.
- Now, after the first boil lower the heat for about 8 or 9 minutes, drain in colander. You should have perfect boiled rice.
- {Tip: When boiling rice always make sure there is plenty of room for expanding and cooking.} Basmati or long grain is the best for any rice dish.
- Try freshly boiled rice with spoonful of butter and sugar, mix and serve.

## Ingredients
### Serves 2

2 cups of rice

¾ full pan of water

1 spoon of sugar

1 spoon of butter

# Kichree

## Method:

- Pour daal into a deep pan, wash it by adding water rubbing with your hands then pour out water, add fresh water and repeat a couple of times.
- This helps if there is any soil bits left.
- Next leave daal in pan with 1 pint water add salt, bring to boil and lower the heat cover with lid, leave for 10/12 minutes.
- At this stage the daal should be at a slightly splitting point to which you add washed rice, stir gently mixing well add water just about half inch over the daal and rice
- Bring to boil and cover with foil, simmer for 15 minutes.
- Once ready add butter, extra butter can be added to individual servings for extra creaminess.
- Serve with yogurt

  {Tip: Always double the amount of rice to each amount of daal}

## Ingredients
### 4/5 SERVINGS

3 cups of rice

1 ½ Cups of green daal

1 level teaspoon salt

Large dollop of butter

# Karri and chaul
## {karri and rice dish}

## Method:

- In a bowl pour besan add 1½ pints of water add salt, huldi, chilli flakes, green chillies, masala, yogurt and ginger. Whisk until smooth, put to one side.
- In a saucepan add oil, on medium heat, fry onions till soft add tomato.
- Next with a masher blend all of the mixture to a pulp.
- {Tip: You can cool mixture and put it through a blender, then back into pan}.
- This will give Karri a smooth texture
- Next, gently lower mixture of besan into the pan and keep stirring all the time until mixture begins to thicken, cook for at least 5/6 minutes add butter.
- Finally, garnish with coriander and serve with plain boiled rice
- See pg120 for rice.

{Tip: Add extra butter to individual serving to give it a rich glossy look and taste.}

{Any tricky words look in glossary.}

## Ingredients
## Serves 2

2 cups besan {gram flour} sifted

1 level teaspoon salt

2 green chillies finely chopped

½teaspoon chilli flakes

1 teaspoon masala

Small piece of ginger crushed

1 medium onion diced finely

2 tablespoons oil

1 level teaspoon huldi

1 fresh tomato

1 tablespoon of yogurt

1 ½pints of water

A large dollop of butter

Coriander for garnish

140

# VEGETARIAN PILAUE

## WITH PEAS OR MIXED VEGETABLES

## Method:

- Wash rice and put aside. To wash, pour into a pan add some water run your fingers through and pour out the water by tilting the pan and holding back the rice, repeat a couple of times till water is quite clear.
- This method of washing and rinsing is getting rid of extra starch, so when cooking, the rice won't get sticky.
- In a deep pan, heat oil and add mix masala, as they seeds start to fry you will be able to smell the aroma, add onions, green chillies.
- Fry onions until soft. Add tomato.
- Fry a little more (poon). Add salt, veg and mix well.
- Poon all ingredients until oil is released and water is dried up.
- Gently lower rice to the mixture and carefully mix well.
- Next, add water ½ inch above the rice.
- Bring to boil and lower heat to very low and cover with foil.
- Leave for 15 minutes on very low heat, remove and garnish with coriander.
- Perfectly, separated grains {vegetable pilau.}

{Tip: Any vegetable can be used, or you can just cook rice with spices only, but remember to reduce the salt.}

{Any tricky words can be looked up in the glossary}

## Ingredients
### 5/6 SERVINGS

3 cups rice

1 small packet of mix vegetables or half packet of peas frozen

1 level teaspoon of salt {See picture pg.

2 tablespoon full oil

3or 4 green chillies sliced in the middle, long ways

1 fresh tomato chopped

Small piece of ginger in strips

1 large pinch of mix masala making sure all spices are included,

{Cardamon, cloves, bay leaf, cumin, cinnamon stick}

Chopped coriander for garnish

# Chicken pilaue

## Method:

- In a deep pan add oil, onion, fry until soft, add 5 mix spices, mix and then add chicken
- Next, stir meat for 3/4 minutes, add salt, chilli powder, green chilli, tomato, sauce, masala and cup of water {poon} for 3/4 minutes.
- When oil is releasing from side of the pan, add washed drained rice, gently stirring it mixing all the flavours
- Then add water ½ inch above the rice.
- Finally, bring rice to boil, cover with foil and lower heat to very low for 15 minutes.
- Garnish with freshly chopped coriander.

## Ingredients

### 4 SERVINGS

2 chicken legs chopped into 4 pieces each

{If preferred boneless use 2 chicken breasts and 1 drumstick}

2 cups of rice

1 ½ teaspoon of salt

1 teaspoon chilli powder

1 teaspoon masala

Large pinch of 5 mix masala {Cloves, cinnamon stick, large cardomn, coriander spice and jeera}

1 medium size onion

1 tomato from tin and sauce

1 green chilli chopped

½ cup of water

Fresh coriander for garnish

# Mitae Chaul {sweet rice}

## Method:

- In a deep pan add water, food colour and washed rice. Boil for 12 minutes, then drain in colander
- Next using a paper towel dry out pan
- Into the same pan on medium heat, add oil, teaspoon of butter and cardomn seeds
- Next, gently add rice and with gentle lifts coat every grain
- Next add sugar and again with gentle lifts coat rice evenly, add butter and cover with foil, lower heat to very low and cook for a further 5/7 minutes
- Finally add flaked almonds

  {Sweet rice is best served hot}

  {Tip: When reheating rice, use microwave, it keeps rice fluffy}

  {Any type of dried fruit or coconut can be added}

## Ingredients
### 3/4 SERVINGS

1 ½ cup of rice

3 pints of water

1 ¼ cup of sugar

1 dessert spoon of orange food colouring

Handful flaked almonds

Pinch of seeds from small cardomn

½ cup of oil

1 teaspoon butter

1 spoonful butter

# KEER {RICE PUDDING WITH PISTACHIO}

## Method:

- In a deep heavy bottom pan add rice and wash a few times until water is almost clear to remove the starch.
- Next pour most of the water out, leaving ½ cup of water in with the rice.
- Place on high heat and gently add milk. Stir, mixing the rice, water and milk
- {Tip: Leaving a table spoon in the pan throughout the cooking process prevents the milk from boiling over}
- Stir every 3/4 minutes to prevent sticking to bottom of pan.
- For the last 5 minutes, using the table spoon, press the rice against the side of the pan to blend into a creamy consistency.
- Finally, take rice off heat and add sugar mixing it evenly.

  Rice Pudding can be eaten hot or cold!

## Ingredients

### SERVES 4

COOKING TIME 35/40 MINS

1 cup of rice

2 pints of milk

½ cup of water

½ cup of crushed pistachios

¾ cup of sugar

# CURRIES

How to Chop a Chicken

Spicy Wings

Mince Kebabs / Burgers

Machi with Chaul {salmon fish with plain boiled rice}

King Prawns with Peppers and Sweet Chilli Sauce

Keema with Peas {mince with peas}

Karai Champa {Dry fried ribs in karai}

Karai Fried Chicken

Chicken, Pork or Lamb with Spinach

Chicken Curry

Dishes Made From Leftover Chicken

Boiled Eggs in Rich Curry Sauce

Tangy Tomato Chicken

Spicy Egg

Oven Roasted Pork/Lamb Ribs

Pork Ribs in Thick Curry Sauce

Easy Full Punjabi Chicken

Diced Pork or Lamb in a Rich Curry Sauce

Fried Egg and Bacon Punjabi Style

Peppers With Bacon

# How to chop a chicken

FOR KARAI CHICKEN, CHICKEN CURRY AND CHICKEN PILAU

## What you need

A wooden chopping board

A sharp knife

A sharp meat cleaver

## Method:

- Place chicken flat on chopping board. Place, your fingers under the joint of leg press back and release joint.
- Next with your knife make a clean cut at the joint. Repeat with other leg.
- Next, place leg flat on board and with cleaver make 1 sharp blow in the middle of the joint, you will now have 2 pieces, a thigh and a drumstick, chop thigh in half and half the drumstick.
- It is your choice if you like to have full piece or small pieces.
- {Tip: Keep pieces reasonable size or you will have tiny bones loose in the sauce and not safe when especially when serving to children}
- Next, place your fingers behind one shoulder, with knife make a clean cut on top of shoulder bone.
- Next, place your thumb in the cut and with your fingers behind and a gentle force, pull away.
- You should have a clean wing and whole breast, repeat with other side.
- Next, slice breast into roughly 1 inch pieces, you will be left with whole wing.
- Slice through joint of wing and you should have 2 pieces, with knife make a cut on the skin and keeping knife steadily cutting into skin, keep rolling wing, repeat with other piece, you should have 4 skinless pieces, wings and joints.
- Place the back of the chicken on board and with cleaver make a sharp blow towards the lower half, now make a sharp blow down the middle, you should have 2 pieces, the rest can be discarded.
- Always wash chicken with cold water, removing any intestines in the back of the chicken.
- Wash hands and always have separate chopping boards for meat, fish and vegetables to avoid cross contamination.

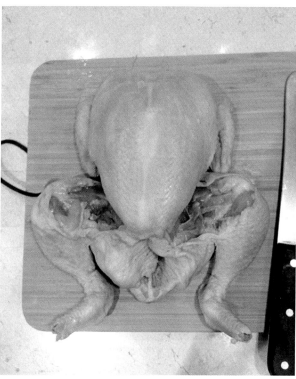
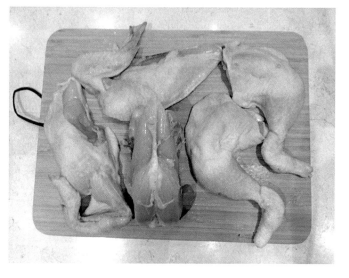

# SPICY WINGS

## Method:

- Take wing and remove skin if preferred
- Place wing on chopping board, with a sharp knife make a cut ,hold knife and keep turning the wing skin easily removed. Wash and drain in collander
- Place wings in a bowl and add salt, chilli powder, lemon juice and half the oil
- Next beat an egg and pour it on to the wings, coat well
- Next in a separate bowl, pour breadcrumbs, tandoori masala, chilli powder  and masala, mix all ingredients .
- Next heat oven 180 degrees, place a roasting dish lined with the rest of the oil
- Next dip each wing in breadcrumbs and place in tray
- Once all wings are in tray cook for 45/50 minutes
- Turning them half  way through cooking process.
- Serve with home made chips.

## Ingredients

12/14 chicken wings

1 teaspoon salt

1 teaspoon chilli powder

1 teaspoon masala

1 dessert spoonful tandoori masala

Squeeze of lemon juice

2 /3 tablespoons of oil

1 egg

3 tablespoons breadcrumbs

# MINCE KEBABS / BURGERS

## Method:

- In a food processor, add all ingredients and mix.
- Next, soak kebab sticks in warm water.
- Take a roasting dish and line it with a thin layer of oil.
- Now take a small amount of mixture and shape it onto a kebab stick.
- Lay kebabs in roasting dish, cover with foil and cook in oven 180 for 20 minutes then turn kebabs and cook for a further 5 minutes.
- Next, remove foil and brown for a further 5/6 minutes.
- Alternatively you can remove them from tray and shallow fry them till golden brown.
- To make burger, line tray with thin layer of oil
- Next, take a round pastry cutter and pour mixture in, pat in down and remove cutter
- You will have a perfectly shaped burger. The thickness will depend on the size of the cutter.
- Cook in oven exactly the same.

   {Tip: Kebabs can be made without skewers - shape them long ways then place them in a roasting tray}

## Ingredients

Packet of mince {chicken/pork/lamb or any meat can be used}

1 teaspoon salt

3 large onions

2 green chillies

Handful coriander

1 spoonful of masala

½ teaspoon chilli powder

Pinch of flour

Kebab sticks

Drizzle of oil

Drizzle of lemon juice

# Machi with Chaul

## {salmon fish with plain boiled rice}

## Method:

- In food processor, put onion, garlic, green chillies, and tomatoes mix and put to one side.
- Next, take salmon pieces and place in a bowl, add salt, chilli powder, huldi and lemon juice rub well onto fish pieces.
- Now, take the mixture from the processor and pour it onto fish gently mix, covering all of the fish, and leave to marinate overnight, or for at least a few hours.
- Once ready to cook .In a karai add oil once heated add jiven, the spice will quickly turn dark that means its ready to add fish.
- Next, lower heat and gently place fish in karai, turn heat to high so fish is sealed.
- Turn over to seal other side, now add the rest of the mixture into karai covering the fish.
- Once all the mixture starts to cook you will see, oil from the sides of the karai, at this stage add 1½ cups of water bring to boil and simmer for a further 2/3 minutes.
- Garnish with fresh coriander; serve with blain boiled rice. {See pg136}

{Tip: Always wash Salmon with cold water and drain for at least 10 minutes before preparing}

## Ingredients

### 6 SERVINGS

6 Salmon steaks about 3 inch wide

Fair pinch of jiven

1 ½ teaspoon of salt

1 ½level teaspoon chilli powder

1 spoonful of huldi

1 green chilli

1 spoon full of masala

1 whole bulb of garlic

Drizzle of lemon juice

1 small onion

½ tin of tomatoes and half the juice

½ cup of oil

Fresh coriander for garnish

# King Prawns

## with peppers and sweet Chilli Sauce

## Method:

- In a pan add oil, fry onions until soft add garlic, ginger, fry until golden brown.
- Add tomatoes and sauce, salt, chilli powder, green chillies mix well
- Next add prawns and turn over for 1-2 minutes till prawns change colour add masala.
- Next, add peppers and whole bottle of sweet chilli sauce and half cup of water.
- Bring to boiling point simmer for a further 2/3 minutes garnish with coriander.
- Serve with naans heated in a toaster, make a pocket add crispy iceberg lettuce add spoonful of prawns. Or you can make a wrap with a roti {See pg104}

## Ingredients

10-12 king prawns washed drained

2 large onions minced fine

6/7 pieces of garlic finely crushed

½ teaspoon salt

½ teaspoon chilli powder

1 inch piece of ginger crushed

1 green chilli finely chopped

½ tin tomatoes and half the sauce

1 ½teaspoon black masala

2 tablespoon of oil

1 spoonful butter

1 cup of water

Sliced half peppers green, yellow and red

Small bottle of sweet chilli sauce

# KEEMA WITH PEAS {MINCE WITH PEAS}

## Method:

- In a pan add oil and onions, fry until soft.
- Next add garlic and fry until golden brown.
- Next add tomatoes and sauce.
- Add salt, chillies, chilli powder and huldi, mix well. With a masher, mash mixture.
- Next, add mince to mixture, coat all the meat, cover and lower the heat.
- Turn mince over every 2/3 minutes, {poon} until oil is releasing from the sides.
- Next add peas and masala, then mix into mince, add 2 cups of water, bring to boil and simmer for 7/8 minutes.

## Ingredients

Any meat can be used besides chicken.

1 small packet    mince meat {fresh mince is better}

2 onions diced

3 pieces of garlic crushed

2 tomatoes and half the sauce

1 teaspoon salt

1 teaspoon of huldi

2 green chillies finely chopped

½ teaspoon chilli powder

1 teaspoon masala

1 cup of peas

2 tablespoons of oil

2 cups of water

Coriander for garnish

# Karai Champa {Dry fried ribs in karai}

## Method:

- In karai heat oil, add ribs, salt and chilli powder. Coat ribs well by turning them over gently.
- Add green chillies and water, cover and leave on low heat for 35/40 minutes checking it from time to time ensuring the ribs are not sticking to karai {If you find ribs are sticking but not fully cooked and they need more time add extra water}
- Once most of the water has evaporated and ribs are partially cooked, add onions and lemon juice then cover for further 3/4 minutes, mix well.
- As onions start to stick to karai, add tomatoes and let it gradually soften by covering it for a further 1 minute.
- Leave karai on gas until tomatoes have turned soft.
- Mix well scraping the karai and collecting the masala of the onions over the ribs. Finally add masala and coriander.
- Serve with lentils dal and plain boiled rice.

{Tip: It is easier to collect and scrape the mixture {masala} made from the onions, tomatoes and green chillies that give the ribs, it's different flavour, to when roasting them}

{Tip: If you find ribs are not fully cooked and falling of the bone add extra water}

## Ingredients
### Serves 2/3

Cooking time: 45 - 60 mins

1 sheet of ribs /or a pack already separated {washed in cold water}

2 large onions finely diced

2 green chillies roughly snapped in half

2medium size fresh tomatoes

1 teaspoon salt

½teaspoon chilli powder

1 ½level teaspoon of masala

Water 1 cup or more if needed {depending how cooked you like the meat}

A few drops of lemon juice

2 tablespoons of oil

Fresh coriander for garnish

# Karai fried chicken

## Method:

- In karai heat oil, add chicken and seal it, add salt, chilli flakes.
- Coat chicken well by turning it over gently; add green chillies, cover and leave on low heat for 5/7 minutes checking it from time to time.
- Once most of the water is all evaporated add onions and lemon juice cover for further 2/3 minutes mix well.
- As onions start to stick to karai, add tomato and let it gradually soften by covering it for a further 1 minute.
- Leave karai on gas till tomato has turned soft.
- Mix well scraping the karai and collecting the masala of the onions over the chicken. Finally add masala and coriander, serve with lentils dal and plain boiled rice.
- {Tip: A whole chicken is better when making karai chicken as it stays moist because of the bones.}
- {This recipe can be made with fillets as well, or after cooking it you can de bone it using your fingers, fillets dry up very quickly so, it is wise to add a thigh or drumstick to give it moisture.}
- Also once cooked and left to cool, it is easier to collect and scrape the mixture {masala} made from the onions, tomatoes and green chillies that give the chicken it's different flavour to when roasting it.

## Ingredients
### SERVES 4

One medium size chicken chopped. see pg . How to chop a chicken

Chop chicken into bite size pieces

2 large onions finely diced

2 green chillies sliced through the middle

2medium size fresh tomatoes

1 teaspoon salt

½ teaspoon chilli flakes

1½ level spoonful of masala

A few drops of lemon juice

2 tablespoons of oil

Fresh coriander for garnish

# CHICKEN, PORK OR LAMB WITH SPINACH

## Method:

- Make chicken, pork or lamb as normal curry.
- Once meat is at stage when oil is releasing add spinach, and all other ingredients mix well.
- Next add 1½ pints of water bring to boil simmer for further 35-40 minutes until meat tender and cooked through and sauce thickens.
- Garnish with coriander.
- Serve with naan bread {see pg120}

    {Tip: Chicken will only need 1 pint of water as it cooks very quickly.}

## Ingredients

1 packet prewashed spinach

½teaspoon salt

½ teaspoon chilli powder

½ teaspoon huldi

½ teaspoon masala

1 tinned tomato and some juice

Piece of diced fresh ginger

2 pints water

# CHICKEN CURRY

## Method:

- Wash chicken and drain, in colander {always make sure chicken is drained completely, because extra water left in chicken will change the way the curry cooks.}
- In a deep pan, add onions, fry on low heat after 2/3 minutes add garlic, and fry more until both are very golden brown.
- {Tip: Whilst frying onions and garlic, add a very tiny pinch of salt, this prevents them sticking to the pan}
- Next, add tomatoes – and sauce, salt, chilli powder, turmeric, ginger, green chillies and mix well, add chicken turn over gently coating all of the meat, and cover.
- Leave on medium heat, every 2/3 minutes lift lid, turn over chicken and cover, this process is called {poonan} use a sturdy tablespoon or a wooden spoon as this helps bring the mixture together.
- Repeating this process for about 5/6 minutes as the water dries out, it is almost ready and as the oil is releasing, add masala and 1½ cups of water bring to the boil and simmer for a further 3/4 minutes take off heat and garnish with coriander.
- Best served with plain boiled rice and chapattis, or homemade golden brown crispy chips.

## Ingredients

2 large fillets diced and 2 pieces of on the bone chicken e.g. drumstick or thigh

{Tip: Adding a piece of bone with the fillet gives a rich texture to the sauce}

3 large onions diced

4/5 pieces of fresh/frozen garlic crushed

A quarter cup of oil

1 teaspoon salt

Huldi one level spoonful

½ teaspoon chilli powder

Black masala tip of tablespoon

2 Green chillies finely chopped

Small piece of ginger {one inch} finely chopped

3 tomatoes from a tin plus half of the juice

Chopped fresh coriander, for garnish

# DISHES MADE FROM LEFTOVER CHICKEN

If you have leftover chicken curry, you could turn it over by simply adding peas or potatoes

## Method:

- Take chicken out of pan and place in a bowl, now in the same pan and without washing it add 2 tablespoon of oil, now add potatoes and the rest of the ingredients except coriander, mix well, coating potatoes add 1½ pints of water bring to boil and simmer for about 10/12 minutes checking every 5minutes until potatoes are cooked through.
- Now take chicken and gently stir it in the pan, add coriander.
- Best served piping hot with cold rotis {See pg104}
- You can use half a packet, about 100g of peas instead of potatoes.

## Ingredients

Leftover chicken curry

2 large potatoes diced roughly about 1 inch

1 level teaspoon salt

Half teaspoon huldi

Level teaspoon chilli powder

1 teaspoon masala

½ tinned tomatoes and some of the juice

1 green chilli chopped

Small piece ginger

# BOILED EGGS IN RICH CURRY SAUCE

## Method:

- Boil eggs, for at least 20 minutes, drain eggs and run them under cold water put them to one side.
- Next, in a deep pan add oil and onions fry till very golden brown add all ingredients except masala and coriander, poon the masala in the pan until it releases oil, add half cup of water, use a masher and blend masala even more to make it smooth.
- {Tip: If you find it hard to do this, then pour masala into a blender and blend it to give it a smooth finish}
- Pour it back into pan and add a further 1½ cups of water bring to boil add black masala and put to one side.
- Shell eggs, and gently shallow fry to give them a crisp coating.
- Slice eggs, long ways and gently place in them in the masala in the pan, use the ladle to cover the eggs by pouring masala on top add coriander leave for at least 1 minute on low heat for eggs to absorb  flavours.

  {Tip: Always shells eggs when masala is ready to prevent eggs changing colour}

  {Any tricky words look in glossary}

## Ingredients
## SERVES 4

8 medium size eggs

3 large onions minced

1 green chilli chopped finely

Piece of ginger chopped

2 tomatoes from a tin and some of the juice

½teaspoon salt

½ teaspoon chilli powder

½teaspoon huldi

1 tablespoon of oil

Plus ½ tablespoon of oil for frying eggs

1 teaspoon masala

Cup of water

Chopped coriander

# Tangy tomato chicken

## Method:

- In a deep pan place onions, fry for 2/3 minutes, add washed drained chicken.
- {Tip: Always wash chicken in cold water and drain it for at least half an hour before cooking, because if its not drained properly it will contain excess water and affect the taste of your dishes.}
- Next, add salt chilli powder, green chillies, tomatoes and sauce.
- Mix well bring to boil, cover and leave it on low heat for 7/10 minutes, checking every 2/3 minutes that it's not sticking to the pan.
- Once all water has evaporated, and oil is releasing from the sides of the pan take it off the heat, add masala and garnish with fresh coriander.
- This dry chicken is great for eating in a Roti Wrap fantastic if you're travelling it beats a sandwich ANY DAY!

## Ingredients

2 large fillets cut into thin strips

3 large onions diced

2 tablespoon full of oil

1 Tin of tomatoes

1 teaspoon salt

2 green chillies roughly cut in half

Large pinch of chilli powder

1 ½ teaspoon masala

Coriander to garnish

# Spicy Egg

## Method:

- In a non-stick frying pan
- {Tip: Use a large frying pan it helps eggs spread better}
- On low heat add margarine and onions, fry until onions are a little brown and soft.
- Next, add ginger and tomatoes fry for 30 seconds or until tomatoes have turned soft, then take pan off heat.
- In a bowl crack eggs, add salt, masala, chilli powder, green chilli and coriander, whisk for 30 seconds.
- Next, put pan back on low heat add mixture slowly folding it, leave it soft and not too dry.
- This spicy egg can be eaten hot or cold, it is good served in a roti wrap.

## Ingredients
### 2/3 SERVINGS

4 Large eggs

1 large onion finely sliced

1 green chilli finely cut

Small piece ginger cut

Fair pinch of chilli powder

Small pinch of salt

Fair pinch of masala

1 small tomato chopped

Big pinch of chopped coriander

1 tablespoon of clarified margarine

# Oven roasted pork/lamb ribs

## Method:

- Wash meat in cool water, and place into a bowl.
- {Tip: Always wash meat with cool or cold water, helps keep the flavour in.}
- Next add salt, chilli powder, masala, tandoori masala, rub well making sure all meat is well coated, and add lemon juice, oil, green chillies, and onions.
- Next pour all into roasting bag and lastly add water. After tying it, shake bag letting every piece to be coated, and place in oven gas mark 180 degrees for 1 hour 20 minutes.
- Now carefully open bag and grill for 2/3 minutes drying up moisture.
- {This method of roasting can be used on diced pork/lamb/chicken or any other meat.} Just remember chicken cooks in 1 hour.
- It is better to let meat marinate for a few hours or overnight.
- Serve with spicy beans and baby roast potatoes.

## Ingredients

1 sheet of ribs / or pack already separated

Spoonful salt

Spoonful of chilli powder

Spoonful tandoori masala

Squeeze of lemon juice

1 teaspoon masala

Drizzle of oil

½ cup of water

1 large onion sliced

2/3 green chillies whole

1 roasting bag

# Pork Ribs in thick curry sauce

## Method:

- In a deep pan add, oil, onions fry for 2/3 mins add garlic, fry until very golden brown
- Add tomatoes, half the sauce, salt, huldi, chilli powder, green chillies and ginger.
- Next, add washed drained ribs and mix well by turning them over every 2/3 mins with all the sauce wrapping the ribs.
- Next, add 1 cup of water to help ribs get pooned keep doing this for a further 4/5 minutes.
- As oil is released add masala and rest of the water bring to boil, cover and simmer for 40/45 minutes or until meat is very tender and nearly falling off the bone.
- Finally, garnish with coriander, serve with homemade chips, salad and hot or cold rotis.

{Tip: Add extra water if you think sauce is a little dry, or if meat needs more cooking time, it depends how you like your meat.}

{Any tricky words look in glossary}

## Ingredients

1 average tray of pork ribs separated and chopped further in half

3 large onions diced

3 /4 cloves of garlic crushed

1 large piece of ginger chopped into small pieces

1 green chilli finely chopped

1 quarter cup of oil.

1 level teaspoon of salt

½ of a tin of tomatoes and half the sauce

½teaspoon of chilli powder

1 level spoonful of black masala

1 cup of water
+ 2 pints of water

# TANDOORI ROAST CHICKEN

## Method:

- Lift skin off the chicken and rub salt sparingly
- Mix tandoori masala with chilli powder lemon juice and oil.
- Rub on to chicken making sure it's all covered by lifting skin.
- {Tip: Leaving skin on chicken, will prevent it drying out}
- Leave to marinate overnight if possible or even few hours; this will help soak in all the flavour.
- Heat oven to 180 degrees. Place chicken, into a pyrex roasting dish, cover with foil, and cook for 1hour.
- Next, turn chicken over, cook for further 20mins, now remove foil and baste with juices from roasting dish repeat process 4/5 times for the next 5/10 mins.
- To check if chicken is cooked through, put skewer in the breast of meat if it comes out almost dry it is done.
- Serve with lentils and roast potatoes.

  {Tip: I find that a Pyrex roasting dish makes a lot of difference when roasting meat than if you roast it in a tin roasting dish, this makes the meat very dry}

  {Tip: Use same method when roasting drumsticks and thighs, place in roasting bag for 50-55 minutes}

## Ingredients

One whole chicken, washed with tale removed

½ Spoonful salt

Chilli powder: 2/3 spoonfuls

Tandoori masala 1spoonful

Lemon Juice

Half cup oil

Foil

# Diced pork or lamb in a rich curry sauce

## Method:

- On a low heat place in a deep pan oil, onions and garlic. Fry until soft and golden brown
- Add green chillies, salt, ginger, chilli powder, huldi and tomatoes with the juice. Stir well making sure all meat is coated with mixture.
- Turn it over every 2/3 minutes {spoon}, repeat process for 5/6 minutes, when it's looking nice and browned and you can see the oil is releasing and all water is almost dried up.
- Next, add pinch of tandoori masala and masala, mix and add water.
- Bring to boil and simmer on very low heat for 25 to 30 minutes or until meat is tender to the touch and sauce has thickened, add extra water if you think it needs more cooking time, garnish with coriander.
- Serve with cold chapattis made a day earlier

  {Tip: Always add masala last, because if you add it in the beginning, it will make your curry look very dark and with a sour taste}

  {Tip: Always add extra garlic when cooking any other meat than chicken especially lamb because it disguises the fresh meaty smell.}

## Ingredients

One small packet of diced pork /lamb or other meat

3 large onions finely chopped

4/5 Cloves of garlic crushed

Small piece of ginger crushed

1 level teaspoon salt

1 green chilli finely chopped

½ teaspoon chilli powder

1 teaspoonful of huldi

1 level spoonful of black masala

Pinch of tandoori masala

3 tomatoes and half the juice from the tin

One quarter cup of oil

One and a half pints of water

186

# Fried egg and bacon Punjabi style

## Method:

- In a frying pan add spoonful oil, pierce green chillies and fry them till they change colour, now remove them from pan and fry bacon.
- Once fried to your liking, crisp or medium add little more oil and fry eggs.
- Next place bacon, eggs in a breakfast plate and sprinkle salt, chilli powder and masala place fried green chillies on top of eggs.
- Serve with roti {chapatti} and taste the difference.

## Ingredients

### SERVES 2

6 slices bacon

4 eggs

2 Green chillies

Salt to taste

Pinch of chilli powder

Pinch of masala

# Peppers with bacon

## Method:

- In karai or deep frying pan add oil and peppers then cover for 10 minutes on low heat until soft and slightly brown, put to one side.
- Next in a separate frying pan add oil and place minced bacon, add chilli powder and cover, leave for 10/15 minutes or until bacon cooks through and all the water released has dried up.
- Next crisp bacon to your liking, then add peppers and masala.
- Lastly take all the contents and pour into a large sieve, draining all the extra oil.
- Serve with lentils and homemade chips.

  {Tip: I have not added salt to this dish as bacon already has salt in it}

  {Bacon is quick to make, alternatively you can use any mince, just remember to add ½ teaspoon salt for other meats.}

## Ingredients

### MAKES 6

3 large peppers sliced in half

1 packet 600g bacon bits

1 tablespoon oil for frying bacon

1 tablespoon oil for frying peppers

1 teaspoon chilli powder

1 teaspoon masala

# TIPS

- Add a pinch of red or orange food colour to give your curries that extra rich look.

- Always add butter to vegetarian dishes, it gives it a creamy texture and taste.

- Make a masala of onions and garlic, freeze it ready for cooking chicken or any other meat when you're in a hurry.

- Boiled rice the night before can be freshened with boiling water poured over.

- Never eat rice that has been left out in room temperature, as this will give you food poisoning.

- When pooning your onions and garlic add a tiny pinch of salt, this prevents onions sticking to pan.

- When grounding garlic with mortar and pestle {dori sota}, add pinch of salt this helps keep garlic together and not jump out.

- Adding salt to dishes when making a masala for curries, use the tip of a ladle or tablespoon and with the eye measurement, it's very easy to roughly judge about a teaspoon or so. Look at picture of example shown on pg12

# Tips

- Masala is another word also used for onions, garlic, tomatoes, salt and spices that are fried pooned} before adding the main ingredient, meat or veg.

- When deep frying, keep karai on back hob, it is safer should there be any spillage.

- When defrosting meat overnight in a fridge, always put it on the bottom shelf, so nothing drips onto other food and cause cross contamination.

- Always use separate chopping boards for meat and veg.

- Always let food cool down to cold, before putting it in a fridge or freezer.

- When making rice pudding, never cover pan. Leave a table spoon in the pan all through the cooking process, this will prevent it boiling over, as you may find milk boils over very quickly if left on hob.

- When reheating rotis in the microwave, wrap them in a clean tea towel, and heat only for 30 seconds. This will keep them soft, if left too long in microwave they will harden very quickly.

- Roti wrap can be eaten buttered or plain

# TIPS

- Corriander can be frozen straight away without chopping it. Once frozen you can take a small amount as it breaks easily. If bought with soil attached at to the roots - soak it in cold water, and by shaking it in the water the soil will release, repeat until water is clear.

- Always bottle freshly ground masala to keep it fresh - it will last longer. {Glass bottles are best at preserving} The aroma will always be strong and inviting.

- Always wash rice with cold water.

- Never waste left over garlic or ginger - it can be frozen in a sealtight container.

- Once you have made dough let it sit for at least 20 minutes before rolling it out.

- If you've added too much salt, add a whole potato to dish whilst cooking.

- When frying any type of pakora make sure heat is low, and always lower what you are going to fry slowly and as closely as possible inside the wok karai. This will prevent any oil splashing back.

- To dry excess water when making sagg, move sagg to the sides of the pan, water will quickly evaporate without burning contents.

# Dishes that compliment eachother

- Lentils and oven fried ribs in a bag and roast potatoes.

- Ronghi {kidney beans} in rich sauce with Karai Chicken and plain boiled rice.

- Machi {salmon} and plain boiled rice.

- Lentils with fried aubergine, fried potato wedges and plain boiled rice.

- Ronghi {kidney beans} in rich sauce with fried bacon, sausages and plain boiled rice.

- Mava di daal, with plain boiled rice plain pakoras and mint chutney.

- Mava di daal, with mixed pakora.

- Lentils, with mixed pakora or plain pakora, mint and imbali {tamarind} chutney.

- Punjabi style roast chicken and spicy beans with any daal, and small roast potatoes.

- Alloo gobi {cauliflower and potato} with Patura {small naans} or prantha {flat fried bread}

- Lentils, toria {ladyfingers} with plain boiled rice, mint and ginger chutney and fried potatoes.

# GLOSSARY - TRANSLATION {PUNJABI - ENLGISH}

Alloo — Potato

Achar — Pickle

Atta — Chappati flour

Batau — Aubergine

Besan — Gram flour, used for curries and pakora batter.

Channae — Chick peas

Daals — Pulses, different types.

Huldi — Turmeric, deep yellow coloured spice. Huldi is also used as medicinal purpose, for cuts and grazes.

Hari murch — Green chillies.

Imbali — Tamarind, sweet and sour fruit for chutneys.

Jeera — Cumin, used for mixing in with other spices to make the original {Masala.} Also used for pilaue and tarka.

Jiven — Spice used for tarka to dhals and fish also for medicinal purpose.

Karai — Two handle, flat and wide, frying pan suitable for frying naans, puri, karai chicken, pakora samosa.

Kali murch — Black peppercorns.

# Glossary - Translation {Punjabi - Enlgish}

| | |
|---|---|
| Kurchi | – Large tablespoon or ladle. |
| Lal murch | – Red chilli powder |
| Lachia | – Cardomns, used for flavouring tea, puddings also masala. {2 types small, green ones and big black ones, called Moti lachi} |
| Longe | – Cloves |
| Methi | – Fenugreek, greens with small leaves like spinach, can be used in pakoras or cooked with potatoes as a veg dish |
| Masala | – Black pepper +5 spices or the main sauce for curries |
| Moti lal murch | – Red chilli flakes, mostly used in when making Sagg |
| Mita Chaul | – Sweet orange coloured rice |
| Noon | – Salt |
| Palak | – Spinach |
| Paturae | – Small fried bread made from self rising flour. |
| Poodna | – Mint |
| Poon | – To keep frying meat, by turning it over every few minutes until oil is released |

# GLOSSARY - TRANSLATION {PUNJABI - ENLGISH}

| | |
|---|---|
| Puri | – Small fried bread |
| Prantha | – Flat fried bread |
| Pyage | – Onions |
| Roti | – Chappati |
| Suchia | – Thin large fried naan bread made with plain flour |
| Tava | – Flat heavy pan, for making chapatti's |
| Tarka | – Livens daals, by frying jeera seeds in butter, and adding to daals |
| Thanyia | – Corriander |
| Tamatar | – Tomataoes |
| Uderak | – Ginger |

# Thank you

I have a lot of people to thank for this book, it would not have been possible if it wasn't for our elders especially my mum and dad, who gave up their dreams to give us a better life. I owe it to them to show we have achieved things, and thanking them for bringing us over here.

They left behind their parents, siblings, their home and the world in which they grew up and loved. I try to imagine if I could have ever done that, I think not!

They was very brave to come to a country with no language communication. I believe it must have taken a lot of thought and courage. With a struggle, brought us from the Punjab to a better world, Aberdeen, Scotland, where we grew up. I would like to thank my mum for teaching me all that I know about cooking.

Every dish is what we cooked in the family kitchen. I have not added any western ingredients to make it different, I have just cooked it my way, and for me practice makes perfect.

I am grateful to the King Street School that gave me the education to read and write. I left school at the age of 10. After we moved from Aberdeen to Glasgow, I was not sent to school and I loved being at home.

But later in life I regretted it so much that after my own children grew up I thought I've got to do something, and went into adult education whilst working as a lunchtime organiser. I trained to become a teaching assistant, and worked with special needs for a few years.

I am currently working at Sedgley Park Primary, thanks to Mr John Gregory {Head of school} for believing in me, and giving me the T.A position. I love my job, it's not like work, as the people around me are like friends {an extended family} plus I love the children, it gives me great pleasure to put a smile on each and every child. It's what makes me happy.

I would like to thank Mark Skelton{y6 teacher}, whilst working and supporting in year 6 I picked up quite a lot as literacy was not my strongest point. I would like to thank Rachel Mistry, who put Word on my laptop and this book began, and her husband Jay Mistry for doing the photos.

I would like to thank my friends and colleagues at school who have encouraged me to write this book, which started as a joke, every time they would ask how something was made I would say "Wait for my cookery book!" and now it has happened. I have surprised myself.

I would like to thank my husband Jasbir, my best friend, who has supported me with my writing all the way, listened and corrected me.

My granddaughter, Neelam, who helped me with my book and some of the photographs.

All my grandchildren for the support they've shown me, Har rai, Kierat, Kirtan, Nihal and Kavan.

My boys Popsi and Amit, my son in law Raja, my daughter and best friend Meena, and my daughter-in-law Teraj. My childhood friend Moira, who helped me decide the title.

I would like to thank the publishers Spiderwize for accepting my book, especially Laura who has guided me through and graphic designer Camilla who has made it happen.

I hope this book will be enjoyed by those who like Indian food but can't cook, YET!

I have tried my best to simplify recipes, easy to follow instructions, tips, should you wish the need to question anything in the book feel free to write to nirmalasingh@hotmail.co.uk

*Nirmala Singh*